I AM ME

By the Oliver Ellsworth School

Publish Your Purpose Press

Publish Your Purpose Press
141 Weston Street, #155
Hartford, CT, 06141

The opinions expressed by the Author are not necessarily those held by Publish Your Purpose Press.

Ordering Information: Quantity sales and special discounts are available on quantity purchases by corporations, associations, and others. For details, contact the publisher at orders@publishyourpurposepress.com.

Edited by: Leslie Wilson
Cover design and interior layout design by: Nelly Murariu

Printed in the United States of America.
ISBN: 978-1-951591-76-2 (paperback)
ISBN: 978-1-951591-77-9 (ebook)

Library of Congress Control Number: 2021909906

First edition, May 2021.

The mission of Publish Your Purpose Press is to discover and publish authors who are striving to make a difference in the world. We give underrepresented voices power and a stage to share their stories, speak their truth, and impact their communities. Do you have a book idea you would like us to consider publishing? Please visit PublishYourPurposePress.com for more information.

CONTENTS

DEDICATION

This book is dedicated to every child
who questions whether they are enough.
You are, and then some. Your story is important.

We also dedicate this book to our
listening adults who take the time to see
the world through children's eyes and
promote inclusion and equity.

DEAR READER,

The Hartford Foundation for Public Giving is the community foundation for the Capitol Region of Connecticut—your community foundation—committed to bringing together resources, both human and financial, to improve the lives of all residents. Our work is only possible through the dedication of our partners: donors, nonprofit agencies, professional advisors, and community and business leaders.

Windsor Public Schools, through the Office of Family and Community Partnership, graciously received COVID Relief Funds in the amount of $75,000 to enhance social-emotional learning and equity through literacy. A portion of the COVID relief funds from the Hartford Foundation for Public Giving was used to sponsor the *I AM ME* social studies book publishing project during the pandemic. In this project, families and students co-design and co-develop with teachers to model how partnerships are constructed and how high-impact engagement strategies are implemented.

The Hartford Foundation for Public Giving supports the project's intention to focus on cultural stories written by families and illustrated by students. Windsor Public School students were able to focus on literacy skills with emphasis on social wellness, cultural identity, and engagement of families and students through writing and illustration. The project allows students to see themselves in what they read and is a wonderful example of the kind of work we want to elevate.

The Windsor Public Schools Office of Family and Community Partnership's (OFCP) vision is to increase student achievement through improved collaborative partnerships and to further develop capacity (skill and understanding) of families, our schools, and our partners. The OFCP proudly supports the opportunity to partner with students, families, and teachers in an effort to **further strengthen skill and understanding through the *I AM ME* Project.**

Sincerely,

Christina L. Morales, *MSW*
Coordinator, Office of Family and Community Partnership/Coordinador, Oficina de Colaboración entre la Familia y la Comunidad

601 Matianuck Avenue
Windsor Ct 06095
Tel: 860.687.2000 Ext. 1284
Visit us: www.windsorct.org
Follow us on
Twitter: @WPSOFCP
Facebook: Windsor Public Schools

**Remember, it's not what happens to you. It's how you handle it. **
***The enemy uses discouragement and doubt to steal our joy and our miracles. Rise up and move forward with encouragement. ***

ABOUT THE FUNDER
Hartford Foundation for Public Giving
Together for Good ®

We are the community foundation for the Capitol Region of Connecticut—your community foundation—committed to bringing together resources, both human and financial, to improve the lives of all residents.

Our work is only possible through the dedication of our partners: donors, nonprofit agencies, professional advisors and community and business leaders.

ABOUT THE I AM ME PROJECT

Oliver Ellsworth school is representative of the diverse world we live in. It is our intent not simply to tolerate diversity but to embrace it. It is our mission to turn diversity into equity and inclusion in every aspect of our practice and our personal lives. This book is meant to be transformational. The stories from our families, students, and faculty will forever change the way we understand one another, inevitably improving our practice, how we live, and how we interpret the world. We will work together to find the beauty in the fabric of our community, cultivating the genius in one another and making the world a better place.

No longer do we need to interpret someone's life from a certain position or way of thinking. Storytelling gives families & staff the ability to express themselves in their own unique ways. It also provides us with a stage that promotes transformative listening, and conversations that will increase our ability to learn and adapt. The *I AM ME* project will provide other benefits we may not discover for years to come. We do know there will be an immediate positive impact for our students and beyond.

ACKNOWLEDGEMENTS

Thank you to everyone in the Oliver Ellsworth Joyful Learning Community who helped make this project possible!

To our parents and students - we thank you for allowing us to tell your stories. We appreciate the time you spent attending our workshops and writing at home as a family. We hope that you found this experience to be meaningful and that you now know how valuable your stories are.

To our amazing Oliver Ellsworth staff - we could not have done this without you! We are fortunate to have staff members who believed in this project and were willing to volunteer their time.

We would also like to give a special shout out to **Principal Gruber, Vice Principal Higgins,** and **our Reading Coach Marcia Ferreira**. Thank you for the love you give to our students, families and staff here at Oliver Ellsworth. You help us dream big and give us the support we need to make the magic happen.

Thank you to **Windsor Public Schools** and **the Office of Family and Community Partnership**. When we needed help getting this project going, you were there for us.

Finally, thank you to the **Hartford Foundation** for believing in and funding our project. It is not every day that young children and their families get to become published authors. We accomplished something amazing together that will have lasting impact within our community.

Those of us who are lucky enough to live and work in this community know how special it is. And now, hopefully YOU our readers will too.

ABOUT OLIVER ELLSWORTH SCHOOL

Oliver Ellsworth School is a pre-kindergarten through second grade school in Windsor, Connecticut, the state's first settled town. Oliver Ellsworth School is rated in the top five percent of most diverse schools in Connecticut.

Diversity, equity, and family and community partnerships are the cornerstones of our success. We at Oliver Ellsworth are a family, devoted to **"cultivating the genius of every child."** We are here to ensure that every student has the knowledge, independence, and self-confidence to succeed as a happy and productive member of society.

We are so proud to share the multitude of perspectives our families' stories present. If students at such a young age can publish a book, we know they can grow to be whatever they want to be.

OUR STORIES

Ryan Brooks
Kindergarten
Rayna Dyton-White and Regina Dyton

RYAN AND REYA

I am **Ryan** and I am five years old. I'm still young. My sister, **Reya**, is nine years old. She's still young, too.

I like to play *Roblox*. I like to play with my sister, but we don't always agree. She thinks pink is ugly, but I like pink. Reya wants me to think pink is the worst color. Reya only likes green and white and black. I don't like her colors at all. Reya thinks My Little Pony is dumb. I love My Little Pony.

Reya and I don't always agree, but **I like my sister and she likes me.**

Reya and me at her school concert.

MY FAMILY

Katie Essex
Grade 2
Margaret Essex

I am **Katie** and I would like to share about my family. I have a mom, a dad, and a little sister named Amanda. We have a dog. His name is Bentley. Amanda and I like to play with Bentley and bring him on walks. Sometimes we walk with our neighbors. Other times we ride our bikes while Mom and Dad walk with Bentley. My sister and I like to help our neighbors fill their bird feeders and clean up their yards.

I sing in the Junior Choir at church. My mom sings in the Adult Choir. Amanda sings in the Cherub Choir. We go to church on YouTube during the Covid pandemic. I can't wait to go back to church in person. We love to visit with our family. I have two grandmas, two grandpas, a Poppy who is my great-grandpa, and aunts and uncles. I like to visit my aunt and uncle who live in Ohio. The rest of my family lives close by.

My mom, dad, sister, and I all do karate. My favorite part of karate is that it makes me stronger. My mom likes to kick and punch. Dad likes to hit the punching bags. Amanda likes doing the karate circuits. We all really like spending time together. We go to Cape Cod every year. We love to go to the beach to play in the sand, collect shells, play with the hermit crabs, walk on the sand flats, and watch the sunset. There is also a beach with big waves!

I love my family and they love me!

This is a picture of my family at Cape Cod in 2019. My Grammy Dale, Grampy Chuck, Uncle Jon, and Aunt LeAirra were with us!

I AM KENDALL

I am **Kendall**.

I am five years old, in kindergarten, and an only child.

I *love* ice cream! I don't like broccoli with cheese.

Even though my cousins live in California, Connecticut, Virginia, and Texas, my family still loves to get together for holidays and special days.

I love my parents and get to see my grandmas every day.

I like playing soccer and board games, going to New Hampshire, and playing at the playground and parks. One day we went to Nantucket; they have the best beaches.

On Nantucket you can see all the stars including Orion's Belt. I want to be an astronaut when I grow up!

My favorite time of year is spring because I get to look for Easter eggs on Easter and it's almost summer.

I am me: silly, happy, and smart.

I am Kendall.

Ice cream is my favorite dessert.
My favorite flavor is mint chocolate chip.

YOU CAN CALL ME ARI

Ariella Trifone
Grade 1
Tracey Zotter

My name is **Ariella**, but my friends call me **Ari** (my Aunt Ally calls me Ella, because that was my great-great-grandma's name). I am in first grade, and my favorite class in school is Art. I love to draw and color. I have a *lot* of pets (1 dog, 4 cats, 2 fish), but my favorite is my dog, Dizzy. We like to sing and dance around the house together, especially to old records (*Ghostbusters* is my favorite). I really like *Pokémon* and playing video games with my family, too. I also like playing with balloons and bubbles, and I have a lot of stuffed animals!

I love my family most of all. My cousins are my favorite friends and I like to visit them as much as I can. I like making them happy and always do my best to make them smile when they are sad. My dad likes to teach me about astronomy. I know all the planets and fun facts, like Jupiter has a red dot in it that could fit three moons! My mom likes to read with me before bed; we really like *Mr. Putter and Tabby* books. **I am happy, I am funny, I am Ariella Nicole Trifone.**

I love to draw. Here is a picture of me and my mom and dad.

Mia Gomez
Pre-K
Purvi Gomez

ME, MY SILLY SELF, AND I

I am **Mia Gomez**. I just turned five and am in preschool. I start kindergarten this fall. I love to spend time with my family. I have an older sister, Emma. We are best friends. We color, play dress-up, and make Play-Doh things together. We pretty much do everything together.

I like to play outside on my playground. I love to collect rocks. I pick up new rocks everywhere I go. I keep them in the car, in my jacket pocket, in my backpack—really anywhere I can fit them! I also love to listen to music and sing. My mommy says I am silly and love to joke around. Sometimes I joke around too much and I get in trouble. I want to be a teacher when I grow up. I am special because I am kind to everyone, caring, smart, beautiful, and one of a kind! **I am Mia Gomez!**

Me being silly while my mommy is trying to take pictures. Me dressed up as Wonder Woman. Pictures of me, my sister, and one with my cousins.

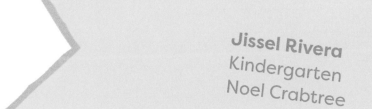

My first day of kindergarten. I was so excited!

I AM LOVED!

Hi! My name is Jissel and I am six. I like this world because it is full of joy. I like helping others because it makes us great. When I help my parents with the house, it makes them happy. I am kind because when I see someone alone, I will play with them. I love my mom and dad, my friends, my family, and my toys. My favorite things are art, recess, soccer, gymnastics, and dance. Also, I like myself because I am really sweet. My mom always tells me that I can do anything I put my mind to. **I know I can do it!**

Jayden Lamoureux
Grade 1
Emily Lamoureux

JAYDEN'S LIFE

My name is **Jayden Lamoureux** and I am seven years old. I love my cat, Amber, and I enjoy buzzarding around. That means I like to have fun and joke! Did you know that my favorite movie is *The Secret Life of Pets*? I also have a great time playing *Mario* video games on the Wii and even created my own game with objects in my home, complete with sound effects.

I am vegan, which means I do not eat animals. I love my family. I play board games, ride bikes, and read books with my mom, Bawa. She helps me with the violin, too. I play ping-pong and watch science shows with my dad. I went to Italy in 2019 and climbed rocks in Cefalu! I am always joking with Mimsy, my grandmother, and I play volleyball with Pa, my grandfather. I like water balloon fights with Dee, my great-aunt. I like playing with my cousins, Brady and Luca. I also enjoy hearing silly cat stories from my great-aunt Ro. **That's just a little bit about me!**

Me with my cat in 2021.

AMAZING ANNIKA

Annika West
Kindergarten
Sasha Aldridge-West

I am me, the **amazing Annika!**

I have a mom, a dad, two older brothers, and a younger brother. I enjoy spending time with my whole family, including my aunts, uncle, and grandparents. We eat together, play games, take walks, and travel to places like Jamaica and Bermuda.

I love everything about school, but I really enjoy learning about Black History. Rosa Parks and Harriet Tubman are my favorites because they did wonderful things for the world!

I just looooove to dance! My mom says I was dancing before I was sitting up. I like to twirl when I dance. I take jazz and tap classes now, but I used to do ballet. **I love my life!**

My Auntie Samantha did a photo shoot of me at the park for my fifth birthday. I was being a lovely lady, wearing my favorite color, pink.

Mason Mclean
Grade 2
Nicole Webster

A MAN IN THE MAKING

I am a man in the making: smart, handsome, and stylish! I am **Mason Mclean**. Let me take you on a journey and show you all the things that make me who I am. The joker, yes, that's me! I make my mom and dad laugh so much. I wear cool glasses and have many pairs. Math is my favorite subject, and I love playing video games. I am seven years old, but my parents told me I have an old soul. I love the skin I am in. My brown complexion means so much to me. I am a young activist, attending rallies and using my voice to create change for people who look like me; they call me the young Martin Luther King.

There are so many sides to who I am, from loving dinosaurs, movies, and playing card games with my family to being flexible and smooth with my karate moves. I have many titles—son, brother, god-brother, grandson, nephew, cousin, friend, gamer, and the most important title, *leader*. Oh—and how could I forget? I call myself a nerd, but not your typical nerd. I'm a fashionable, loveable, popular, well liked, smart, and friendly nerd.

I am Mason Mclean. My aesthetic and personality shine bright, from my futuristic glasses to my Marvel cameo character shirt and jacket. This is me, a man in the making!

My dad says, "Nerds get all the girls." Ha ha! I think I get my jokes from him! No girls for me right now. I'm focusing on growing up and being the best man I can be, just like my dad. My dream is to one day become an engineer and create my own video games. I am loving myself and learning how to become a man. These are all the things that make me who I am and what is creating **the man in the making, me, Mason Mclean.**

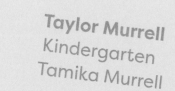

A CHAT WITH TAYLOR

Playtime fun.

I AM ME! I am imaginative! I love spending time with my best friend, my big sister. I love playing dolls with her and performing for my family and friends. I have at least twenty doll friends and counting. I enjoy going shopping. Shopping is my delight. I am always excited to walk down the aisles and see all the new toys.

I am loving. I love my family and give them kisses and hugs every day. I like to take care of them and help all the time. My family makes every Friday night family movie night. I make homemade pizza with my mother on Friday nights. My family likes to travel. Every summer, we take trips near and far in search of fun in the sun and new adventures.

I am so many things! I am imaginative. I am loving. I like to travel with my family and I am a shopaholic. **I am Taylor!**

Adam Cardwell
Pre-K
Marc Cardwell

This is a green goblin and its monster friend.

I CAN MAKE SO MANY THINGS!

Hello! My name is **Adam**, and I'm creative! That means I like to make lots of things. I like drawing cars, robots, and other cool things like yetis and monsters! I also like drawing rhinos because they have pointy horns. I love to draw with a yellow highlighter in the art notebook that Daddy gave me. I also like to make pictures of our family with colored pencils and markers. My favorite colors are brown, olive green, and "normal" green. "Normal" green is not dark and not light—it's both!

I like cooking *arepas* with Daddy. *Arepas* are my favorite Venezuelan food. They are kind of like sandwiches made of cornmeal. You can put lots of different foods in *arepas*, but I like putting cheese in mine. I also like putting in chicken, because chicken is healthy. I also like to make banana tacos with Mommy and my sisters! I like building and painting plastic models with Daddy. My favorite things to paint are pink goblins! I like making snowmen. First, roll a giant ball. Next, you roll a medium-sized ball. Then you make a small ball for the head. Finally, you add two rock eyes, or coal eyes, or button eyes. Finally, you add a carrot nose!

I love making Sofi, my baby sister, laugh. She laughs when I do silly things, like when I pretend my hand is a bug on my head! Sometimes, I do a handstand on the couch and use the back of the couch to hold myself up (because I'm still learning how to balance)! One day, when I am older, I want to learn how to carve things out of wood. I would make lots of things, like birdhouses.

The End.

MY FAMILY IS SPECIAL TO ME!

Jaden Trowers
Grade 1
Gwen Trowers

I love myself and I love my family.
My family is like a circle and I can feel love from everyone.

I like when we gather for holiday dinners and parties. I help with baking the cakes, pies and cookies.

I love Mommy, Daddy, Sista, Tony, and Jakai. I also love my other relatives.

I miss them when I'm at school with my Oliver Ellsworth family.

Here is my family. We are very tall and happy.

Aiden Ricketts
Grade 1
Shauna Whitter

I am a six-year-old autistic young boy. I love being outdoors and riding the carousel.

I AM AIDEN

On, April 8, 2014, at 8:06 p.m., I came into the world. My name is **Aiden Omar Ricketts**. I was born in Hartford, Connecticut U.S.A to two Jamaican parents, Shauna and Omar. The doctors told my parents that I was the most beautiful baby they had ever delivered. My mom described me as a nocturnal baby. My dad pronounced me a future heartbreaker. Who am I? Well, I am an autistic six-year-old who sees the world differently from others. I enjoy each moment of the day as if there is no tomorrow. I let everyone do the worrying, while I live life with no worries. I like to do risky things and when reprimanded I smirk or laugh out loud. I sometimes wonder why everyone overreacts so much. I love to do things on my time; however, I cooperate with others.

I am the youngest for my mom and dad. I have one older brother on my mom's side and two older brothers and three older sisters on my dad's side. I live with my mom, step-dad, and big brother. I love music; I have a harmonica, a piano, and a flute recorder. I make music in my spare time.

I love outdoor activities. When I am outdoors, I am in my element and I run freely and explore everything around me. My favorite outdoor place is the playscape. I can play on it for hours and hours if allowed to. I enjoy being the center of attention. I am very energetic and stay busy all day until it's time for bed. I go to Oliver Ellsworth and I am in first grade. **I love my school and my classmates.**

ME AND MY FAMILY: THE TANKSLEY'S

Jiani Tanksley
Grade 2
Chanae' and Jamaal Tanksley

My name is **Jiani Kennedy Tanksley**. My dad picked my first name. My middle name is after my grandfather, Kenny, who passed away. I live in Windsor, Connecticut with my mom, my dad, and my newborn baby sister, Jayla. Guess what! I picked my sister's first name. Her middle name is Ruby, after our 97-year-old grandmother!

My family identifies as Black, African American. My family loves our culture. We have learned that we come from queens and kings. My family enjoys learning about Black peoples' strengths. My mom loves to do our hair in unique styles with braids, beads, or afros.

My family enjoys spending time together. On Friday nights we order pizza and watch a movie or play cards or games. We are very competitive, and I *hate* to lose.

**I love my family.
We are the best!**

friday family fun night playing cards!

I AM GIANNA MARTIN

I am **Gianna "Gigi" Nicole Martin**. I *love* my brown skin! I am beautiful, smart, brave, and

funny. I love dancing. I started doing tap at two years old. I now do tap, jazz, and hip-hop. Hip-hop is my favorite. I also love sports. I even played football and was the only girl on the team. I was really good.

I love my family so much. I have two big brothers, DJ and Makai. We are also a military family. My mom was in the Army and Airforce, and my dad is still in the Army.

When I grow up, I want to be a pilot and fly airplanes. I will call my airplane "Gigi's Airplane" because **BLACK GIRLS ROCK.**

Gianna's family photo.

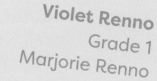

Violet Renno
Grade 1
Marjorie Renno

These are pictures of me on my adventures and some of my drawings. Every day is a new day for me as I try to be kind and learn new stuff.

A RECIPE FOR VIOLET

My name is **Violet**. Would you like to cook with me? You will need one cup of bravery, twenty ounces of looking for adventure, some Italian seasoning, and a bit of Irish luck with a sprinkle of Scottish fluff. Then, get a bucketful of sugar for my sweet tooth. You will also need a heart full of kindness, a dash of art, and a bushel of gardening. Don't forget to throw in my awards for reading and growing sunflowers. You will need at least 21 girl scout badges and a scoop of Legos. Crack one veterinarian egg on top because that's what I want to be. Now you must Mix It! Shake It! Stir It! And Dance! Last, pour out the cookie batter, shape it, and bake it in a dragon's fire. Serve it on your favorite *Pokémon* card and enjoy **your Violet Cookie Concoction!**

Isaiah Hestick
Grade PreK
Allison Hestick

I AM ISAIAH!

This is a picture of me enjoying the spring weather outside.

Hi! My name is **Isaiah**. I am a fun-loving four-year-old!

I love my mommy, my daddy, and my twin brother Isaac.

My favorite thing to eat is a peanut butter and jelly sandwich with a spoonful of Nutella... mmm, yummy!

I love to use Magnatiles and Legos to make fun creations such as castles or a forts.

I also like to use boxes to build things such as a race car that I can actually fit into and pretend to drive.

I love to visit my grandparents' house on the weekends to watch family movies.

I like to play internet games, and *Roblox* is one of my favorites because **I can build and create things.**

Janan Brown
Kindergarten
Olivia Brown

BEING A FRIEND TO ALL

I am **Janan**. I am nice because I always make time for my friends. I give the greatest hugs but have to do air hugs for now because of coronavirus.

I help Mommy play video games so we can save the princess together. Sometimes I go to Grandma's house to make waffles or pancakes. The pancakes are so soft and buttery; I can taste them right now! I wish I could share them with all my school friends someday.

My friends at home are my ponies and dolls. I always welcome the new ones with special meals and games.

My mommy says being friendly is my gift. **I hope I can make a hundred friends so I can play with them.**

Janan likes to get all her favorite toys together to celebrate new arrivals. Her favorites are ponies and dolls.

Gabrielle Williams
Grade 1
Hillary Williams

I love being home with my family.

ALL ABOUT GABRIELLE MARIA

My family can be described as loving. I am seven years old and a first-grader. I have a twin sister and two brothers.

I share a bunk bed with my twin sister, Beverly. My name is Gabrielle which means "woman of God." I love to read and play basketball. My first word was "dada." Kevin is my daddy's name. He teaches us math and history almost every day. My mommy's name is Hillary. She teaches us reading and good manners. I am going to be a teacher when I grow up.

My favorite colors are black and red. **I love my family.**

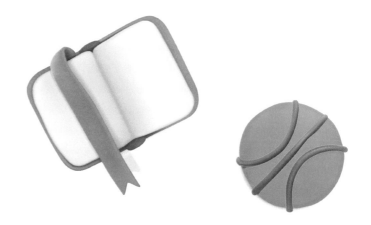

This is my favorite thing to do: draw!

BEVERLY THE ARTIST

I am creative and kind. My name is **Beverly**, and I love art. I want to be an artist when I get older. I have two brothers and a twin sister named Gabrielle. We were born five minutes apart, but my lucky number is seven. My dad is named Kevin. He was born in Jamaica. He is a history teacher but is good at art like me. My mom is named Hillary and she hangs my art in her classroom.

Art makes me happy, and I can draw almost anything.

Graycie Giacomazzi
Grade 1
Laurie Giacomazzi

GRAYCIE ROSE

I am very good at gymnastics. I also like to dance. I do jazz, ballet, and tap.

My family has lots of pets. My favorite pet is my black lab, Rocky. He is a therapy dog. I like to watch movies with my family.

I also like to go to the beach. My favorite foods are pizza and slice-and-bake chocolate chip cookies.

Now you know all about me!

My dog Rocky and me.

WHO IS KENDALL MAYS?

Kendall Mays
Grade 2
Rachel Mays

Who is Kendall Mays? I will tell you who I am! I am an eight-year-old girl who loves her animals! I mean, I *love* animals. I love animals so much that I take veterinarian classes with the town vet. I hope to become a veterinarian someday. I also love space. I love to read all about space exploration and the really cool MARS projects they have. I also want to work for NASA someday as a space exploration scientist. Maybe I can do both?!

I love my astronaut suit! It is the same kind of astronaut suit that Neil Armstrong wore when he did his NASA training.

I love to learn and read books, especially about dwarf planets. I like to read nonfiction so I can learn new facts. I have two dogs. One dog is Pixie; she is a ten-year-old Shichon. I also have a German Shepherd puppy, Rocky. He is just eight months old. I love playing with my dogs! They are so much fun! I also love cats! I know a lot about cats. I secretly hope that my aunt and uncle will get me a kitty.

So, I have to say, I have the best family. We laugh a lot! My dad is really funny. He tells the best jokes. Everyone loves my dad because he is the dad who will always help you and play with you. The dogs really like his bald head. Mom and I like to cook and bake together. I love my brother! He is the best big brother and really smart. My mom and dad say that I am very kind. I think I am, too. They also say that I am very compassionate. I care a lot about people and want everyone to love each other and to be happy!

In the summer, I love going to the beach! Jumping the waves and swimming in the ocean is my favorite! It is always great when I get to cover up my mom, dad, and brother in the sand. I really love to make sandcastles, too.

This is just a little bit about me, Kendall Mays! Who are you?

Kellen Craig
Grade 1
Katelyn Craig

THERE IS A BOY I KNOW

There's a boy I know with bright blue eyes and freckles on his cheeks. He is kind and a friend to all. He is a brother with a big caring heart that makes us so proud. He is confident and brave with every new thing he tries. He is strong-willed, yet funny, and he is always making people laugh. He is a soccer star who plays with passion. He will create magic with Legos and design creatures with slime. He loves adventure and nature and being in the waves at the ocean. **His name is Kellen, and he is our wonderful son.**

Kellen getting ready for soccer practice this fall.

ALL ABOUT MILO

Milo Battistoni
Grade 1
Cara Battistoni

I am me. I am **Milo Russell Battistoni.** I am seven years old, in first grade, and I'm very tall. I have two brothers who are shorter and younger than me. Their names are Luca David and Theo Dominic. I like being a big brother because I basically always get to be the boss around here. You can find me playing outside with my trucks, riding my bike around Loomis, or playing sports. I want to do a lot of things in my life when I grow up, like join the FBI, be a builder, work as an architect, and serve in the Marines and the Coast Guard.

I am really good at math and love learning about the past, especially about wars and sports history. Jackie Robinson is my favorite biography subject because he tackled challenges and was a problem-solver just like me! I think I am very funny. I make up my own jokes. My dad says they are pretty good. I am happy. I am strong. I love my school! **I am me.**

This is me being silly with my brothers. I'm the big one!

Jaxon Stafford
Grade 1
Erica Fitzgerald

The first box is what I look like. The second box is me and my mom walking our dog, Rubble. The third box is me helping someone who's hurt. And the fourth box is me jumping on the bed.

JAXON'S WONDERFUL LIFE

My name is **Jaxon Michael Stafford**. My middle name comes from my grandfather's name. I love to help people. If they get hurt, I can help them. If they fall and don't have scratches, I can tell them to shake it off. That's what my mom tells me. I have a lot of people in my family whom I love, including my Mom, my Dad, Jordan, and Rubble. Rubble is my dog. We like to ask Rubble if he wants to go on a walk. He goes crazy at the start. We do our walks on days when it's nice out. I like to bring my scooter. **I have a wonderful life with people who make me happy, and I love it.**

Vacation at Great Wolf Lodge in Massachusetts with SheShe, Cameron, Aunt Nicole, Logan, and me.

Kyle Banks, Jr.
Grade 2
Kyle Banks, Sr.

THE JOURNEY NAMED KJ

This journey is all about me, **Kyle R. Banks, Jr.** Some call me KJ. I live with my dad but go to my mom's on weekends. I love to play video games with my dad, ride my jeep and my bike, and go bowling. I enjoy going on vacation with my Aunt Nicole, my cousins Logan and Cameron, and my grandmother SheShe. I am brave, kind, friendly, and a good helper. I want to be an astronaut and go to Mars and the Moon. I went to the New England Air Museum and bought a helmet. My Uncle Karl bought me a fishing rod. He will teach me how to fish this summer. **My favorite TV shows are *Spongebob* and *Ryan's Mystery Playdate.***

Emma Gomez
Kindergarten
Purvi Gomez

ALL ABOUT ME

I am **Emma Gomez**. I am in first grade. My family is the most important thing to me. My mommy is a nurse, and my daddy does ultrasounds of people's hearts. I go to my grandma' s house every Saturday. I call her Mom. Mom teaches me how to make an Indian bread called *Bhakri*. She lets me roll the dough and then she cooks it.

I like to play with my little sister, Mia. We swim, play outside, and ride our bikes. We like to play dress-up and wear makeup.

When I grow up, I want to be a paleontologist, because I love to learn about dinosaurs.

I am special because I am smart, loving, caring, and beautiful. **I am Emma Gomez!**

These are pictures of me and my family. We are at a beach in Newport, Rhode Island, and walking the Cliff Walk. A picture of Snapchat fun and me riding my bike.

CAMPING AND FRIED PLANTAINS

Zadie McMahon
Kindergarten
Rashida McMahon

I am **Zadie Monáe McMahon**. I was named after the writer Zadie Smith. I am in kindergarten and I can't wait to be six years old. I love my family. I have one older brother, Odarion, and one younger sister, Zuri. My dad cooks my favorite food for me every week: salmon and fried plantains! Yummy!

On the weekends, my family loves going to restaurants and having dance parties. I love to ride my scooter and go to the playground. When my dad was younger, he ran track in Jamaica. My mom is from St. Croix. She loves to read and is a professor at Wesleyan. **I want to be an astronaut when I grow up and go camping all the time!**

Zadie is sitting at her distance learning desk. She is in Mrs. Chapple's kindergarten class. Zadie loves to wear her pink glasses for fun.

Erin Fraysier
Kindergarten
Julie Fraysier

I AM IN KINDERGARTEN

Hi, my name is **Erin.** I am going to write about myself.

My favorite thing about kindergarten is snack time. I like math. I like writing. I also like lunch.

I like tacos. I *love* pasta. My favorite time is eating dinner in our back yard!

I feel special because I have a disco ball. **My mom says I am special because I am loved.**

This is a picture of me on my sixth birthday, at Menchie's.

Morgan J Avery
Grade 1
Heidi Avery

THIS IS ME

My name is **Morgan J. Avery**. I am a seven-year- old boy who loves to make everyone smile and laugh.

I have a lot of fun hobbies which include: clay figure making, Lego building, painting, and so much more.

I also like music and doing my silly dance. I love to play video games with my cousins. I love swimming in the pool or going to the beach. When I grow up, I want to be a builder. I love playing dinosaurs with Daddy and building my Lego city with Mommy. **There are so many amazing things in this world that I can't wait to see and do!**

These are some of my favorite hobbies, Legos and clay. It's so much fun!

Julian Santintmoe
Grade 2
San Tint & Moe Muyar Naing

I AM JULIAN

The picture was taken at the pagoda on my way back to Myanmar.

I am a silly guy named Julian Santintmoe. At home, my family calls me Juju. I make fun things and make my family laugh. I am so happy when I see them laughing with me.

My mom gave birth to me at Michael Douglas Hospital in Dover, New Hampshire. I have a sister who is 13 months younger than me. My parents have always told me to take care of my little sister. My family is so special to me because they love me and they do a lot of things for me.

My mom and dad immigrated to the United States from the same Asian country. It is known as Myanmar. The people in the area speak Burmese. My mom worked as a flight attendant in Myanmar for many years. Now she is busy guiding us with our schoolwork and kitchen chores. My dad is always busy with work and studying for his MBA. He took us to his school campus. He plays boxing with me when he has free time. That is my favorite memory with my dad.

I love cars and I have a good knowledge of them. I love to learn about cars on Google and YouTube. My favorite car is a Tesla, and I want to be a car designer when I grow up. I also like to learn about my parents' home country.

Every night, my mom tells me a story about her culture and country of origin. During our summer break, we spent a month with family there. There are many beautiful temples and pagodas. I marked this place as pagoda country. In Myanmar, we visited monasteries and pagodas with relatives. We also went to an orphanage and donated some of our childhood clothes and toys. I did so many exciting things with my cousins. It was the best time of the year for me. I love traveling and want travel all around the world. **I like new experiences and love to learn different languages. That's my dream!**

I AM CINDY

This is **Cindy Santintmoe**. She is very sweet and kindhearted. She loves animals and flowers. She likes to wear only boy's clothes. She doesn't like feminine dress at all. She seemed to like the clothes her older brother wore.

She is warm and very friendly with family, but it is not easy for her to talk with outsiders. Cindy was shy when she attended preschool and kindergarten. She seems to take some time to get comfortable around new people.

Cindy has a balanced mind and loves the truth. And she always has good thoughts for others. She is pragmatic and believes in her own ideas. That's why I think her courageous and realistic responses to her surroundings are a positive sign for her future. **She wants to be a successful businesswoman when she grows up.**

Cindy Santintmoe
Grade 1
San Tint & Moe Muyar Naing

I am Cindy Santintmoe.
I love to take natural photos.

I AM ASA

I am **Asa Anthony Douglas**. I am six years old, and my birthday is on July 17th, which is one of my favorite days. I am sitting in my kitchen writing this story with my dad. We eat chicken every Monday in our kitchen. My grandpa usually cooks it on the grill. Although I love chicken Mondays, my favorite food is chicken nuggets. I live with my grandma, grandpa, mom, dad, and sister.
My sister is named Carrie, but I call her Sissy. She is going to the University of Hartford in the fall. When I grow up, I want to play in the NFL. I currently play flag football and love it. Last year, my team won the championship. My favorite place to go on vacation is Jamaica. My dad was born there, and my mom was born in America.
I love my family and friends.

This is me drawing a fake Nintendo Switch. I made this because I didn't have a real Switch, and I wanted one!

Kimble Nesmith
Grade 2
Aixa B. Couvertier-Nesmith

MY BIG DREAMS

My name is **Kimble Nesmith**. I am seven years old, and when I grow up, I want to be an astronaut and an author/illustrator. I want to be an astronaut because I have always wanted to see the earth from space. I think it would look really cool. (*And* I want to get off this corona virus-filled planet!) I want to know how fast it feels when you take off in a spaceship. I've seen pictures and videos of that on the news. One time, me and my family went outside and saw the International Space Station from our yard. The International Space Station looked like a little red dot in the sky from Earth. When I grow up, I want to be in that Space Station! I want to have fun floating around.

I want to be an author and illustrator, too! I am a huge Dav Pilkey fan. There is a lot of action in his books, and I like action! I have made my own *Dog Man* and *Captain Underpants* books. I am good at art. In my second-grade art class, my work was in the art show! In my old school, I learned to draw a body and not just legs coming out of a head! I started drawing better since that day! I need to keep doing my art in art class so I can get better. When I grow up, I want to create my own book character: CatMan! I got that idea from the *Tom and Jerry* movie. I showed one of my books to my teacher and she loved it! My parents love my books, too!

I want to be an astronaut and an author/illustrator. I know I can do these things and **follow my dreams!**

Sadie Romboldi
Grade 2
Elizabeth Romboldi

I AM SADIE

Hi, I am **Sadie**. I am eight and I am in second grade at OE. I am moving to New Hampshire, so next year I will be going to a different school called Beaver Meadow.

I am nice and smart. I like to play *Fortnite* and *Roblox* with my friends.

I like to eat strawberries and ice cream. I love to draw, and I love art class. I love math and science.

I love space. When I grow up, I want to be an astronaut.

I have one brother and one dog, but no sisters. My brother and I are funny and both love to build Legos and play basketball.

My family is my mom, Elizabeth; my dad, James; my older brother, Mason; and my Shichon dog, Oreo. **My family and I like to tell jokes, tell stories, play games, and celebrate holidays.**

This is my family on our family picture day.
My dad is holding Oreo. My mom is behind my dad.
I'm next to him. My brother, Mason, is next to my dog.

A GIRL NAMED MAURICEA AND HER FAMILY

Mauricea Gordon
Grade 2
Viviene Robinson

My name is **Mauricea**. I am sometimes called Moe-Moe by my mom or Rece by my dad. Let me tell you a little about myself. I am seven years old. I am a unique and very special little girl with a lot of diversity, as I come from three different races. I am part Indian, part black, and part white, so I have a lot of different cultures in me. The Indian and black sides of me come from both my mom's and my dad's families. My dad's family is mostly Indian. My mom's grandpa was Indian, too. The white part of me is solely from my dad's father. He was half black and half white.

Do you know I have a big family? Actually, two families made into one. There is my mom, my grandma, my older sister, and my older brother. Then there is my dad, my stepmom, my three other older sisters, and my three other older brothers. I have eight siblings in total and I am the baby. Let me tell you a secret. *Shhhhh!* I have nieces and nephews that are much older than me. When I was smaller, they would all lift me up and carry me around.

This was my sister's graduation from high school during the pandemic. There is my mom, my grandma, my sister, and me.

I live at two different houses. My permanent address is at my mom's house, but every other weekend and most of the summer I'm at my dad's house. My last birthday was at my mom's house where both my families came together and celebrated me.

Now you see why I am unique and special, I have so much to get but so much to give. **I feel strong and invincible like Wonder Woman.** Bye for now!

Tate Drummond
Grade 1
Nardia Reid

I HAVE AN ANGEL FOR A SISTER

My favorite holiday is Christmas.

This past Christmas was extra special because my dad and my stepmom told me that I was going to be a big brother.

They gave me a cool big brother cape, with a big brother mask and a big brother story book. I felt like a superhero.

I was so happy and excited to soon have a baby sister.

I picked out books to read and games to play.

I even colored some pictures for her.

I just knew that I was going to be the best big brother ever.

One night, my stepmom came to my house and was very sad. That's when my mommy told me that my baby sister passed away and went to heaven.

Superhero and a big brother for my baby sister in heaven.

I was very, very sad because I didn't get to meet my sister. I wanted to name her Butterfly Flower because I think butterflies and flowers are pretty.

Her name is Aria Drummond, and even though I didn't get to meet her, I still feel lucky because now I have an angel for a baby sister.

This is a picture of me
enjoying the sun in my front yard.

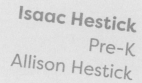

Isaac Hestick
Pre-K
Allison Hestick

I AM ISAAC!

Hi! My name is **Isaac**. and I am me! I enjoy using Legos and Magnatiles to build awesome creations such as giant castles or fast race cars.

My favorite thing to eat for dinner is rice, but I also love spicy foods such as curried chicken.

I love playing with my twin brother, Isaiah! We play tag, hide and seek, and other fun games together.

I love spending time outside hiking in different parks or riding a bike or ATV in my back yard.

I like to visit my grandparents' house, and when the weather is nice we roast marshmallows and make s'mores outside.

My mom and dad are very special to me. I love giving them big, warm hugs!

Jacob Watson
Grade 1
Sagine Alexandre-Watson

I AM JACOB

My name is **Jacob Watson**. I am six years old. My mom is Haitian, and my dad is Jamaican. I was born American. My sister is Jada, and she plays lacrosse. My brother, Jordan, goes to UConn. I like to play basketball, soccer, football, and lacrosse. I really love obstacle courses because they can be a challenge. Maybe I'll be the next *American Ninja*. One thing I know is that I am not going to fall in the water!

My favorite saying is, "I wish I had a machine that could do…" This machine would do everything, especially things that I don't want to do or maybe something that I want. Maybe I will become an inventor to create this machine. I don't know yet. I have a lot of planning to do. **In the meantime, I will create an obstacle course to improve my skills for** *American Ninja.*

I have some tricks.
Check out my moves on my Hoverboard.

I AM A BUILDER

Sahrenity McCloud
Grade 1
Kim McCloud

I am **Sahrenity**, a little brown girl. I like to laugh and spend time with my family. I am curious. I like to learn about how things work, and I really like to build things. I especially like building houses out of Amazon boxes— the larger, the better. I tell my mom I'm going to be a construction worker. She smiles. My dad says I'm a lot like him when he was my age. He built pillow forts. I love to build pillow forts, too!

Building forts requires lots of pillows. I get them from all over our house. My mom reminds me that I'll have to clean them up later. I know, I say as I build the walls. My dad loves my forts. Sometimes he helps. I like that. I even laugh when he knocks over a wall. He is big and tall. He says I'm going to be an engineer. Mom smiles and says I'm full of potential and will be an amazing woman.

I have "Black Girl Magic" like Kamala Harris, Mae Jemison, Beyoncé, Misty Copeland, and Simone Biles. Our class learned about other great women like Ruth Bader Ginsburg, Anne Cole Lowe, Augusta Savage, and Malala Yousafzai. Our teacher, Ms. D'Errico, taught us how these women helped people and the world. Today I am six and I build forts. But when I grow up, I will build and create things to help people, to help our world. I will sing and dance, making people smile and feel happy. I will be an activist to help things change for all people. I will explore this world and beyond. My mom says I can help build our world into a better place. I smile. **I am Sahrenity, and I am a builder.**

I am Sahrenity (the builder).
This is my family picture with my mom and dad.

Joshua Wilson
Grade 1
Rosanna Wilson

MY FAVORITE THINGS

My name is **Joshua**, and I am six years old, soon to be seven! I live with my mom, my dad, and my little sister, Izzy.

I am so lucky because I get to see my grandparents every day. I have such a great family! We do so many fun things.

My favorite things are riding my zip line, watching movies on Friday Family Fun night, going to Cape Cod, and playing with my cousins. My favorite movie is *Raya and the Last Dragon*.

I like to play the piano and I love being outdoors. My favorite colors are green and blue. I love to draw and paint.

Maybe someday I will be artist like my art teacher, Ms. Sloan.

Washington Park is one of my favorite places to go.
I love looking for turtles and fish in the water.
The playground is lots of fun too!

ABOUT MY WONDERFUL FAMILY

Isabella Savelli
Grade 2
Melanie R. Savelli

My name is Isabella, and I have two younger twin brothers named Dominic and Luca. Luca likes monster trucks, so when he grows up, he wants to buy one. Dominic likes playing video games and the piano, so I think he'll do one of those things when he grows up. When I grow up, I would like to be an astronomer. I really like stars and want to study them. My dad knows a lot about stars and has been teaching me about them. I also like cooking and baking with my mom and dad. My favorite things to cook are *empanadas* with my mom and crabbies with my dad. I enjoy working on big puzzles with Grandma and looking at bird houses with Grandpa. Most of all, I like spending time with my family.

In the summertime, we all get into my dad's convertible and drive to get ice cream. Another thing I like to do in the summer is swim with my cousin Maddie Moo in her pool. It's so cold that I always say "brr" when I dip my toe in. When I dip my toe in the pool at Grandma and Grandpa's house, it's toasty warm. Dominic, Luca, my cousins Madison and Patrick, and I love jumping in the pool and getting the toys that sink to the bottom. The best is when it's time to take a break from swimming because Grandma and Grandpa always have treats for us that are so yummy!

I'm so lucky that I have a great family!

My family and two cousins are happy and jumping on a trampoline.

Alyssa Greenwood
Grade 2
Brooke Greenwood

THE BEST FAMILY

My name is **Alyssa**, but at home my parents and younger sister call me Alys. I have a loving, silly, close family. My favorite day of the week is Sunday because my mom and dad make chocolate chip pancakes and bacon! They are awesome cooks. But what I look forward to the most is enjoying summers down in Rhode Island with my grandparents, Popi and Nana. We get to go to the beach and the pond every day and have treats from the ice cream truck that comes by the bungalow. My parents used to call it the music truck so I would not know that it had ice cream!

I think my family is cool because my aunt and uncle are Olympic snowboard champions and my grandfather, Gampy, is a famous photographer known for his ballet images. That is where I come in. I love to dance! I have

Pictures of me doing the things that I love to do: skiing, dancing, and going to the beach. There are also pictures of my whole family—my mom, dad, and little sister.

been taking ballet since I was three, which is most of my life if you think about it. I have even been on stage in a production of *The Nutcracker*. Everyone asks what I want to be when I grow up and I tell them I want to be a ballerina and veterinarian. I think I can do both because my parents tell me that I can do anything if I work hard and am happy. My whole family supports, encourages, and loves me and my sister. **That's all a little girl can ask for!**

I LOVE FAMILY TIME!

Ezra Burke
Grade 1
Kirkpatrick Burke

My family and I spend quality time together.

We go to church together. I love to dress up in the suits my mommy buys for me. I like to sing, dance, and clap my hands. I also like to preach for my family. I even have my own microphone. I like to turn the volume up as far as it can go! I sing gospel songs I hear on the radio and songs that I've written myself.

We play games together. I like to play board games and card games. One of my favorite things to do is play basketball with my brother and my dad. We have a really high hoop, just like the ones in the NBA.

I love being outdoors. I like to gather sticks and tap them on the ground while I make musical sounds with my mouth. I really love going for walks in my neighborhood! I wave at my neighbors as I walk by their homes. Sometimes I get to pet a friendly doggie. I love to run ahead of my mom and dad, but they always tell me to stop or slow down when I get too far away.

I love writing stories and books. I write about cars, church, and superheroes! I am the author and illustrator of my books, though sometimes I ask my dad to draw parts of the stories.

I love when my mom takes me to the mall. She buys me tasty treats and I usually get a new stuffed animal. I have so many on my bed now. My favorite stuffed animal is Bear Bear. I got him from the hospital when I broke my arm. Bear Bear's arm was broken, too, just like mine. We are both better now.

This is me, my mom, my dad, and my big brother. We are all dressed up for holiday pictures.

We eat dinner together every day. On the weekends we eat with our extended family and have lots of fun sharing stories and laughing together.

I am me and I love my family, and my family loves me!

Mason Moauro
Grade 1
Tara Moauro

Me, my glasses, and my bodyguard brother, Tyler.

WHEN I LOOK THROUGH MY GLASSES

When I was two, everything looked blurry, so **I got glasses.** As soon as I put my glasses on, everything was clear and anything was possible!

I could see the movies I love to watch so much better. Playing video games became so much easier... I actually became really good! When I play soccer, I have special sports goggles to wear that help me see the ball. I feel like they give me superpowers and make me score. The only thing I can't wear my glasses for is jumping on the trampoline. My mommy and daddy said they might break if I keep them on.

With my glasses on, I can see everything that makes my family special.

My brother, Tyler, is my only sibling. He is two years older but still plays with me all the time. He is like my own personal bodyguard and is always making sure that I am okay.

My dad is really cool. I want to be just like him someday. He always plays with us and helps me win my video games. He's a corrections officer and makes sure nobody breaks out of jail. Even though I want to be just like my dad, I think I'll be a doctor instead.

Through my glasses I can see all of the hard work my mom does. She helps me get ready for school every day, always makes me lunch, and still works her regular job, too! She's really creative and always draws and plays with me.

My glasses help me see my two dogs. Baily is my four-year-old Husky/German Shepherd. She has one blue eye and one brown eye. She's a lot of fun and even let me ride her down the stairs once. My mommy and daddy said, "Never again!" Jenny is twelve and is a Beagle/Pitbull mix. She makes me laugh because she clucks like a chicken every time someone walks by our house.

When I was little, I was worried about getting glasses, but my parents helped me see how much better everything would be if I wore them, and they were right! **Without my glasses, I wouldn't be me and might miss out on seeing how lucky I am to have the family that I have been given.**

NOAH'S FAMILY

My family is the **Reynolds family**. In my family, I have Dad, Mom, Noah, Ellie, and my new puppy, Charlie.

My Dad is Justin and he sings to me and my sister at bedtime. My favorite song that he sings is "The Cat Came Back." My mom is Mandie and she loves to cook us all yummy dinners. My mom also plays board games and baseball with me. My sister Ellie is two years old and is cute and snuggly. I love playing with Ellie outside. Charlie is my new puppy and is nine weeks old. He is soft and cuddly. He does like to bark a lot.

I am Noah and I am going to be six years old. I am kind and silly. I love playing baseball and making music on my guitar.

This is my family and we love being together.

My family.

Aiden Rodriguez
Grade 1
Christine Rodriguez

AIDEN'S LANDSCAPING

I have big plans for when I grow up. Even though I am only seven, I know exactly what I want to do: be a landscaper! Ever since I was really little, I have always loved watching people mow lawns, especially my dad. I have a mini-John Deere mower and follow my dad around on my tractor every weekend when he mows our lawn.

Not only do I like mowing, but I like watering plants, taking down trees, weed-whacking, and leaf-blowing. Basically, anything related to yard work! I am going to need many things to do it, such as a zero-turn lawn mower, a truck, a trailer, a skid steer, and a stump grinder. I've even figured out a name for my landscaping business: *Loggin' Mowin'*. The name means I can take care of not just mowing your lawn, but taking down your trees, too, if you need me to. **I hope people call me to do a job for them!** I will be there in no time at all.

Me on my tractor.

I AM...

I am **Jeremiah Xavier Chase**.

I am five years old.

I am in kindergarten.

I am in kindergarten during COVID, may I add!

I am adventurous and I love to explore.

I am kind and always willing to share.

I am brave, but I can get scared sometimes, too.

I am athletic.

I am sweet and love to cuddle with my mommy.

I am responsible. I have chores. like feeding my cat, Koda.

I am loved, I have a very diverse family.

I am intelligent and crave learning new things.

I am sensitive (very sensitive; I am a Cancer)

I am musical. I love to sing and play on my piano at home.

I am grateful.

I am blessed.

I am Jeremiah Xavier Chase.

Jeremiah Chase
Kindergarten
Tyler-Simone Thomas

This is me when I was taking pictures with my mommy. I loved all the flowers. I got to explore the nature at the park we were at. Mommy even let me get dirty in my white shirt after the pictures were done.

Chloe Whittemore
Grade 1
Debra Whittemore

MY LIFE AND FAMILY

Hello! My name is **Chloe**. My family has five people in it, and I have two siblings. I like to play outside with my neighbors. I have a pet cat. Our house was built before World War II. In my family, we go on walks and watch TV together. I like that my family is very nice and we all have different personalities. I am energy combined with happiness and perseverance. When I grow up, I want to be a scientist, astronaut, ballerina, and artist, and also work for the Red Cross. **I will help people in need, I will donate things, and I will still have free time to spend with my family.**

Chloe running and playing outside.

FAMILY FUN TIMES

My name is **Isaiah Minnifield**. I have a big, big family. I have a mom and a dad. I have six brothers and two sisters. I am part of a blended family. Do you want to hear a coincidence? Two of my brothers have the same name! I also have lots of aunts and cousins, and a couple of grandmas, too.

My mom and dad are the coolest. They make sure I have food, clothes, and a place to stay. My dad loves to play frisbee and basketball with me. My mom loves to play Uno and checkers. I like to play chess, but mom does not know how to play. I am going to teach her one day.

I am the youngest of all the siblings. Some of my siblings live very far away and some live close by. I do different activities with each of them. Some like to play basketball, some like to work out, some like to read books, some like to play hide and seek, and some like to play video games. They can be bossy because they think I am the smallest. Sometimes I can be bossy, too.

My auntie takes me to karate every Saturday. It's so much fun. My favorite thing to do in karate is punch and kick, but we don't kick or punch anyone—it's just the air. She buys me lunch from McDonald's before she takes me home. I just love McDonald's.

My family is the best and they love me so much. Everyone always takes time to make me feel special and do lots of things with me. **I just love my family! They are great! How about you?**

Isaiah Minnifield
Grade 1
Dorothy Minnifield

This is some of my family. We are having lots and lots of fun. I enjoy spending time with them.

Zali Penny
Grade 2
Tameko Penny

Awwww, I'm so cute...
My first-grade
picture. It's adorable.

SUPER ZALI

I am **Zali** and I'm seven years old. I was born in December 2013. I'm a girl and I'm good at singing and dancing. My favorite animals are puppies and unicorns. My family loves to keep me safe, especially my mom. I love to be helpful because I love people and interacting with them. I have one stepbrother, three stepsisters, and one stepmom.

I'm good at writing poems. I love to write them all the time, and I love me for being me, and I feel special. My last name is Penny and that makes me feel special because I like Abraham Lincoln and we share a coin. I had a dog named Pepe, but unfortunately, she died when I was four. Kind of sad, but I think about her every day.

I really like Harry Potter movies. My favorite characters are Hermione and Harry. I also really like bugs, but not the ones that are gross... You know what I mean. I love butterflies, and I love my mom and my whole family. I love doing funny things and playing jokes on my mom, dad, brother, and sisters. **I like being in this book because I am me, Super Zali!**

WHAT IT FEELS LIKE TO BE ME!

Arielle Kennedy
Kindergarten
Terry Kennedy

My name is **Arielle Zaire Kennedy**. I am in kindergarten. Here is a story about my family. I have an older sister who is 17 years old and a younger brother who is one year old. Where does that leave me? It makes me the middle child, and boy, does it suck being the middle child. I call it the middle child syndrome. My mom is always paying attention to my older sister regarding her grades in school. My little brother gets into everything—I mean lots and lots of trouble. Where does that leave me? *Stuck* in the middle.

Well, if anyone would like to know, I like dancing and listening to music. I like playing with my OMG dolls and different games on my tablet. My sister used to play a game with me that I made up called Neighbors, but now she no longer plays with me. My little brother takes up all the attention, and sometimes I get sad. But I know my family loves me because they tell me every day. **This is how it feels to be me, the middle child. I am Arielle!**

from left to right: This is a picture of my sister Ariana, myself, and then my younger brother Jakai. We love each other. I love my family so very much. This is me!

Kamila Mendoza
Grade 1
Karen Mendoza

FAMILY TIME

I am **Kamila Grace**! My family is so special. I live with my mom, my dad, my little brother, Nico, and my grandparents. We are Puerto Rican. My family speaks English and Spanish. We love to hang out together.

My favorite thing is hanging out with my cousins in the summer. I hear our laughter echo against the house in our back yard. We love eating pizza together. **Having family time makes me happy.**

I love my family:
my mom, dad, me,
and my brother Nico.

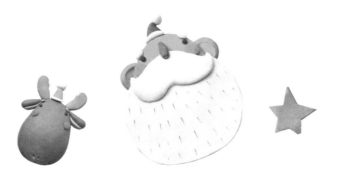

Me and my family.

I AM MAKAI MARTIN

I am **Makai James Martin**. I am athletic. I play football, basketball, and soccer. I also take hip-hop dance classes. I am so athletic that in one of my football games, I had three touchdowns and two interceptions because I am awesome.

I love my family. I am very funny and love to tell jokes. I always try to make my big brother Andre and my little sister Gianna laugh. **My favorite holiday is Christmas and my favorite food is rice and chicken.** I have a bunk bed in my room for my sister and me, and she has two beds in her room so we can have sleepovers all the time.

Zachary Tustin
Grade K
Shawna Tustin

ME AND MY FAMILY

My name is Zachary. I am six years old and in kindergarten. I am in jiu-jitsu and just earned my yellow belt! I love jiu-jitsu and will be able to compete once Covid is over. I want to learn how to speak Japanese; I already know how to count to ten! I also play baseball and want to try football in the fall.

I have two sisters. My eight-year-old sister has a medium-sized bedroom and my oldest sister has a huge bedroom. It's not fair, because she took over our family room! I have the smallest room, but I still like it. My mom and dad sometimes take us out for family days. They are very special and so much fun. We go to a lot of different places. I have two grandmas and one Yia Yia, and one great-grandma named Mimi. I also have two Papas: Papa Food and Papa Tom. I call Papa Food that because he always gives me and my sisters candy. I have lots of

This is my family. It's my mom, dad, sisters, and me.

uncles and aunts and lots of girl cousins. I have one boy cousin but there are too many girls! Unkie is my favorite uncle. I love to visit him, but he lives far away so I don't see him a lot.

I love to spend time in Vermont with my Yia Yia and my cousins and some aunts and uncles. I spent the Fourth of July with Papa Food, my Grammy, my little baby cousin, and some more aunts and Unkie. I also go on vacation with my Grammy and Papa Tom and another aunt and uncle. I love spending time with my whole family. **My family is very big and very special. I feel so happy when I am with them.**

I AM ELIANA GRACE CAMPBELL

Eliana Campbell
Grade 1
Claudia Campbell

My name is **Eliana Grace** but people just call me **Ellie**; that is my nickname. I have a twin sister named Nia Isabel, and we are both in first grade. We live at home with our mommy and daddy, but some people call them Claudia and Andrew. In our family, we love to hug each other and to celebrate God. Our family motto is to "Love hard, speak joy, keep it real, celebrate God."

I love to watch movies with my family and to bake with my mom. My favorite foods to eat are meatballs, pizza, and apples, but not all together. My parents were born in Jamaica. My grandparents, aunts, uncles, and cousins still live there. My favorite holidays are Easter and Christmas because sometimes we get to celebrate all together with everyone in our entire family.

I am special because I am unique and there is nobody like me. I am a gift from God, and I love to make people happy. **My biggest dream is that everyone in the world would be kind to each other and that they would love each other.**

This is a picture of my family. My dad is hugging me, and my mom is hugging Nia. It is my favorite because we hug each other and laugh all the time. We took this picture in a beautiful sunflower field.

Mayra Almodovar Hernandez
Grade 1
Waleska Hernandez

ALL ABOUT MAYRA'S LIFE

Hi, my name is **Mayra Almodovar Hernandez**. I am seven years old and I am in the first grade at Oliver Ellsworth school.

My mom and dad are from Puerto Rico.

I have a sister, and her name is Jalissa.

I know three different languages: Spanish, English, and American Sign Language.

I like art, watching TV, and playing with my sister.

I am at my school, Oliver Ellsworth.

Jayde Vassell
Grade 1
Jonathan Vassell

Washing my go-kart.

I AM PRINCESS JAYDE VASSELL

I am **Jayde Vassell.** I am named after my mother, Janice Vassell, known to everyone as Jay. In my family I am the princess. Ask my parents and my brothers—they'll confirm. My favorite things to do when I'm not bothering my brothers are riding my go-kart, riding my bicycle, practicing roller skating, and watching YouTube on my tablet. My bedroom is my palace, which is painted pink (my favorite color, of course), and in my palace I'm acknowledged as Princess Jayde.

My favorite place to eat is Popeyes Chicken or McDonald's.

Bailey Ceasar
Grade 1
Tamika Ceasar

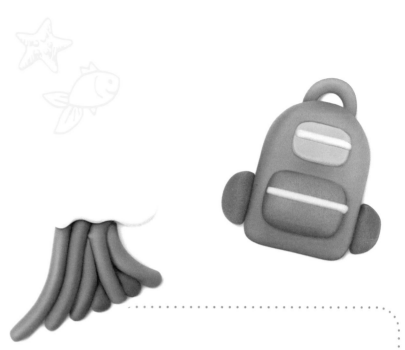

INSIDE THE LIFE OF BAILEY ROSE

My name is **Bailey Rose Ceasar**. I have a mom and dad and a brother named TJ. In October of 2020, I started learning how to play the violin. I also really enjoy gymnastics; I am very flexible which allows me to do cool moves. Arts/crafts and science are my favorite subjects. I have been to the science center at least thirty times. In the summer, I love swimming at the pool in my back yard. I recently became a scout and am learning a lot of new things. Before I go to bed at night, I think about what I want to dream about.

One of my dreams is to someday be president of the United States of America.

Here is my family. My mom asked me to make her look pretty so I gave my mom a flowered shirt. I gave my dad and brother Nike shirts. I gave myself my signature ponytail puffs and a pink skirt.

WE ARE WE

Lincoln Fineman
Kindergarten
Bonnie Fineman

We are we. Just like every family, we have hopes and dreams, fears and worries. We have dinner together each night, trying to keep the kids seated. Then, we give up. We go for ice cream on Tuesday nights. We order sushi on Wednesdays—always the same order—and every week we request "gluten free soy sauce only," and every week we find regular soy sauce in the bag.

We are we. We are a typical family, if there is such a thing. We do laundry—lots and lots and lots of laundry. Our socks disappear in the dryer. We let the kids watch TV for too long sometimes. We go for bike rides, swing from monkey bars, and shop at Costco. We get skinned knees and sore throats. Sometimes, we need time without each other, even if that means pretending to robotically sweep up dead leaves in the corner of the garage.

We are we—just like you. We worry when our boys run a fever or fall and bump their heads. We hung up our babies' ultrasound pictures on the fridge with little star magnets. We inspected them for every finger and freckle. We waited for the first gurgling cries, the first steps, the first words because we are we, and we are the collective "you." We woke up hundreds of times in the night and put a hand on their backs, just to make sure they were still breathing.

One of us has been to war. We are patriots and we are progressives. We love chocolate. We like to surprise friends with unexpected gifts. We are we, yet so many people see us as "different;" in some places, the laws don't protect us because our boys have two moms. Our sons may get questions and strange looks. Our boys have brought immense joy and, like in all families, they create endless trails of dirty footprints across every rug. **People forget that we are we, that we are them. But we are.**

Like many families, we love spending a day in the park in October. We play in the fall leaves and appreciate the last of the mild weather before the snow comes.

Isabella Watkis
Kindergarten
Christina Johnson

MY FAMILY AND ME

My family loves me. I have fun with my family. We watch movies together, bake cookies, read, and play together. Inside, we play cards, Legos, dolls, BINGO, video games, Connect 4, and other board games. Outside, we play basketball, keep away, and volleyball. We ride bikes, jump rope, catch, play in the snow, and enjoy nice walks. We read books together on most days and every night.

My family is nice and fun. I love them. They look out for me. I am special because I am unique. **I know that I am loved because of my family.**

These are snapshots of fun moments with me and my family: my mom, dad, and big sister.

MY GREAT-GREAT-GREAT AUNTS

Damaia Simpson
Kindergarten
Aleasha Macklin

I am **Damaia**, but my family calls me My-My. I have a *big* family! We love to be around each other and we try to see each other often by having cookouts, parties, and celebrations. I have two great-great-great aunts, as well. Aunt Johnnie Mae is 84 years old; she was born in 1937 in Americas, Georgia. She and her family moved to Connecticut in 1944 when she was seven years old. Aunt Johnnie Mae is the second oldest out of nine children. She worked as a nurse's assistant at a hospital until she retired in 1997. Aunt Johnnie Mae has three children and is a grandmother and great-grandmother. She loves to tell stories and to talk about the past!

Can you believe that I also have an aunt who is 105? Her name is Aunt Mary Jane! She was born in 1919 in Americas, Georgia, and relocated to Connecticut with her siblings when she was a young adult . Aunt Mary Jane is the second oldest out of six children. She worked many different jobs before she retired from her last job at a convalescent home. Aunt Mary Jane is a mother, grandmother, and great-grandmother. The many things Aunt Mary Jane has lived to see are incredible! So much history and so many stories to tell. Do you want to hear something pretty cool? Aunt Mary Jane is Aunt Johnnie Mae's ... aunt! I **love my family and my great-great-great aunts!**

Aunt Johnnie Mae is kissing my hand in the top middle picture. She loves giving out kisses! Aunt Mary Jane held me a lot when I was a baby. My little sister Damaria is in the top right picture.

Lauren Fraysier
Grade 2
Julie Fraysier

ADVENTURESOME

Hi, my name is **Lauren**. I like to do crafts and art and play outside. I'm shy around people I don't know, but I like talking to people I do know.

My favorite foods are cheeseburgers and French fries. They're really good.

I like to go camping with my friends and family. I also like being active and kind.

When I grow up, I want to go around the whole world—except the coldest part of the world and the hottest part of the world.

I like dogs and puppies. They're so cute!

I am adventurous!

Did you know dogs can live to be over twenty years old?

Disney World is in florida.

french fries and cheeseburgers are often bought at McDonalds.

I AM BRANDEN

I was talking about my future and about when I have my own plane.

I am **Branden Rattigan**. I was named after my grandparents and great-grandfather.

I am West Indian and I love my family. I am one of 27 great-grandchildren. We spend a lot of time together as a family for holidays, and every month we celebrate someone's birthday.

I am unique, and my mother calls me King because I am powerful and smart. She says that I can do anything and that I make her and my father proud. My favorite movie is *Black Panther*.

I am an inventor, so I can make great things for the world to be a better place. My hobbies are riding my bike and reading.

I want to be a pilot so I can fly my plane anywhere in the world. **My plane will always have fresh strawberries since that is my favorite fruit. I love being me!**

Alanni Ayala

Grade 1

ShaNequa Buchanon

I AM ALANNI

Amazing, lovable, ambitious, nice, nifty, intelligent.
I am Alanni.
I am a first-grader.
I am seven.
I am Alanni.
I am sweet like chocolate.
I am Daddy's girl.
I am the princess.
I am Alanni.
I imagine unicorns on the beach while watching the sunset.
I hear ocean waves through sea shells.
I am Alanni.
I dream to be a teacher and help children learn.
I want them to enjoy school as much as I do.
I am Alanni.
I believe in always trying your best and never giving up.
Learning is a journey and not race.
I am Alanni.
I am a daughter, sister, and granddaughter.
I am from Mommy and Daddy.
They are from Gammy and Grandma Dolly who love me.
I am Alanni.

I am from making ice cream out of snow and building snowmen, and waking up to a snow day.
I am from playing tag and racing in the yard, swinging at the park and blowing bubbles.
I am Alanni.
I am from camping in the summer, swimming in the lake, and s'mores by the fire.
I am from backyard barbecues and Pho Sundays.
I am from Soca music and the Electric slide. But I also love the traditional Indian-style music with Grandma.
I am Alanni.
I am from chicken curry and homemade macaroni and cheese.
I am from a family who loves to cook.
I am Alanni.
I am from movie nights and building forts with my little brother.
I am from taking care of my puppy like a baby doll.
I am Alanni.
I am from *Hair Like Mine* & I am enough.
I am from *Family Reunion* and *Victorious*.
I am from love and memories.
I am Alanni Faith Ayala.
I am Alanni.

A girl like me, Alanni Ayala. This is me.

I AM J.R.

I am **J.R.** My whole name is James Ricci Fitzsimmons. My name is special because I am named after my grandfather (my dad's father), Poppy, and my great-grandfather (my mom's grandfather), Papa. My grandfather Poppy is named James. And my great-grandfather's family name, when they came over from Italy, was Ricci.

Family and being together are important in our house. I live with my mom and dad and my older sisters Mia and Stella. And we have a dog named Quari (short for Quarantine). My sisters have special family names, too. Mia's middle name is Keane, which is my Grammy's (mom's grandmother's) maiden name. Keane is also my mom's middle name. Stella's middle name is Smith. That was my great-grandma's (dad's grandma's) last name. I think it is special to remember our family and be reminded of them every day when we say their names.

My family is also special because we enjoy spending a lot of time together. We moved from our house to my Papa and Grammy's house to help take care of them. In the mornings, everyone would be asleep except me and Papa. We would share special treats like eclairs. My great-grandparents passed away, but I loved helping and learning from them.

My family eats dinner together almost every night, and we share about our days. In the summer we have cookouts and play whiffle ball and kickball in the back yard. If we are not outside, sometimes we have dance parties in the dining room. My mom is a dance teacher, and we all love to dance. Except maybe dad, but he tries. We always find fun things to do together, and we have

special traditions. Every year on the day before school starts and on the last day of school, we have ice cream for dinner! The day after Thanksgiving, we always decorate for Christmas and watch *Elf*. For our birthdays, we ask our friends to bring food instead of presents so we can donate to the Windsor Food Bank. I learned from my family it is important to care and help others. And we continue family traditions from my Grammy. For St. Patrick's Day we make her special scones and Irish soda bread. She came here from Ireland as a teenager.

I think having a close family is special. They teach me things and help me whenever I need it. And I help them and teach them things, too. We work together and help each other. **And we try always to remember how special it is to be together.**

J.R.'s special family.

Dezaree Foster
Grade 2
Jocelyn Knight

I AM DEZAREE FOSTER

This is me, Dezaree Foster. I was dressed fancy for the Daddy-Daughter Dance!

Hello, everyone. My name is **Dezaree**. I am eight years old and in the second grade. I live with my parents and my younger sister. I am polite and delightful, as my grandparents would say. I am special in my very own way. I love the color purple and my favorite furry friend is Panda. I love spending time with my family. Cooking and baking together at The Big Dipper Diner (my special name for my grandma's kitchen) are fun times for me.

I love to ride my scooter and my bike. Going on adventures is what I like! Summertime is my favorite season. I love to vacation with my extended family. We go to beaches and amusement parks together, and we have fun in all types of weather! Swimming is my favorite sport, whether in the back yard or at a fancy resort. I like horseback riding with my grandpa and also singing in the church choir. **When I grow up, who knows what I'll be? Maybe a fashion designer or race car driver is the path for me!**

I AM JANELLE FOSTER

Janelle Foster
Grade 1
Jocelyn Knight

I am **Janelle**. This is all about me. I am six years old and in the first grade. I live with my mommy and daddy and big sister.

I am unique and full of spirit. My favorite color is pink. I love to wear dresses each day, even when I go outside to play.

My grandparents call me Little Miss Princess! I am sassy, some might say. I'm not afraid to do things my way. I am kind and loving to all my friends and family. Enjoying special times with them is what I love most. I'm lucky that they all live so close!

Holidays are my favorite time of the year. We all get together and spread holiday cheer. Playing video games with my sister and cousins, and Nana's cooking, are the best! And my dad always likes to put new recipes to the test.

When I grow up, maybe I'll become a famous ballerina! I love to dance and can imagine filling up an entire arena!

This is me, happy as can be! Always remember to chase your dreams!

Kharissa Thomas
Grade 2
Sasha-Gaye Tinker-Thomas

THE DIARY OF A BEAUTIFUL BROWN GIRL

Kharissa being happy.

HI, hi, hi. My name is (drumroll, please!) **Kharissa**! I am seven years old, and I am very cool. Yes, I said it, I'm the coolest! I laugh when I am happy, I cry when I'm sad. I love to play with my friends, and that makes me very glad. I like to PAARTAY! It is my favorite way to pass the time. Yes, that's right!

Sometimes I feel like a fairy and sometimes I feel like a queen—which, by the way, I think is pretty neat. My zodiac sign is a Leo, and I also think that is very cool. Someday, want to be a famous YouTuber with my name in lights. Wow, would that be great! You see, I am just a regular seven-year-old with regular dreams, only I'm brown like bark on a tree. I just want to be heard, I want to matter, I want to be someone people admire.

The End.

Do Do Do DOOO Do Do YA!

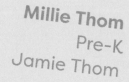

Millie Thom
Pre-K
Jamie Thom

ADVENTURES OF MILLIE BEANZ

Millie and Mommy at The Edge NYC.

My name is **Millie** and I am five years old. I like to travel and go on adventures with my mommy. I have been to the San Diego Zoo, Roger Williams Zoo, Disneyland, and Disney World. I have gone to games at many stadiums, including Fenway Park, Soldier Field, Wrigley Field, Lambeau Field, Yankee Stadium, Notre Dame Stadium, and Lincoln Financial Field, to name a few. I even got to travel on a huge cruise ship that made stops in Mexico, Jamaica, and the Dominican Republic.

I like spending time at my Nana & Pop's house in Florida and going to the beach. One of my favorite places to visit is New York City. There is an American Girl store there and lots of tall buildings with amazing views. It is such a fun city. **I can't wait to see where my adventures will take me next.**

Xavier Kyle Williams
Grade 1
Kimberley Williams

I love being in nature, with mom and Amir. I love waterfalls and riverside and beaches.

X IS FOR XAVIER

My name is **Xavier Kyle Williams**. I am in first grade and I play the cello with Waylon, and I practice at home so I can play better every time. My favorite type of music is *all* music! Michael Jackson is my favorite singer. I also like watching and listening to the music videos of Bruno Mars. I love having dance parties with my mom and little brother, Amir. We turn the music on super loud and get our wiggles out.

At school, I play Monster with my best friend Zack, and I choose him out of all my classmates to come with me to the peanut-free table. I like to make silly jokes and make others laugh. I love eating chocolate. I love to do cartwheels and aerials and I push myself to the limits. I love to play on the trampoline where I can practice all my tricks.

Outside is my favorite place to be, exploring nature, taking long hikes with mom and Amir, and digging for earthworms, I've always wondered what they eat. I love spring, summer, and fall, and although I do not like winter, I love to play in the snow.

My family is from Jamaica, I have visited there three times before. It is super warm and always feels like spring or summer. I love going to the beaches there and visiting my many aunts, uncles, cousins, and grandparents.

My family has taught me to give hugs, love myself, and always show love. Sometimes Amir gets in my space, but I still love him. He loves building forts and I like to help break them, but it's always nice when we watch movies together underneath them first. We like to play *Robin Hood*, with bows and arrows made from clothes hangers.

At bedtime we read a Psalm with Grandma and say our prayers and pray for toys and sweets. Then we cuddle with mommy for nighttime TV before we close our eyes to sleep, knowing that the next day is full of more adventures.

THE FOX AND THE PUPPY

Armando Bernardino
Grade 1
Jennifer Bernardino

Once upon a time, there was a fox and a puppy. The puppy saw the fox. The fox saw the puppy. They wanted to be friends. The fox's dad said, "No, don't be friends. The puppy could hurt you." The puppy's mom said, "Don't be friends, because the fox could eat you". Once, the fox and puppy snuck outside in the cold dark night to play. Then the puppy's mom woke up and said, "Don't be friends, because the fox could scratch you." Then the fox's dad woke up and said, "Don't be friends, because he could bite you." The fox and the puppy were determined to be friends. Finally, late in the afternoon when they were running in the forest, they made a promise to always be friends. **They would continue to be friends everlasting.**

This is me, Armando. I have a special power: I can do a split! I broke my arm on my scooter. That is why I am wearing a cast.

Bijou Analo
Grade 2
JoAnne Analo

I AM AN EQUESTRIAN

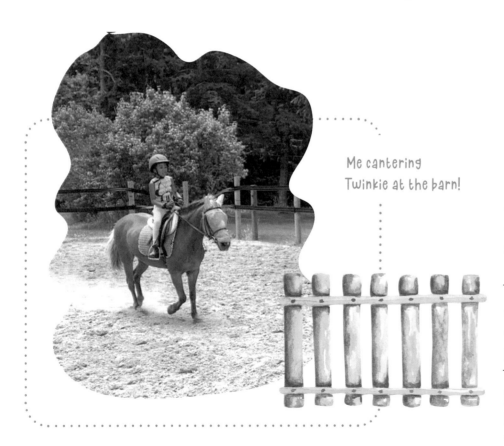

Me cantering Twinkie at the barn!

My mom: My mom is nice, kind, and funny. She works at UConn. My brother: My bro is nice, funny, and he *loves* pizza and McDonald's. My grandma: She is nice, kind, and she loves me, and I love her (same for my mom and brother). I love my whole family.

My family made me the Awesome Bijou! I am special because I am talented. I have many skills, but my favorite is my horseback riding. I am an equestrian. I have a horse named Twinkie. I spend most of my weekends with him at the barn. Sometimes I visit him during the week, too. When I am having a great riding day, I can canter, meaning we jump instead of run. That's my favorite thing to do with Twinkie! He really likes walking when he's tired out. **I hope when I'm older Twinkie and I will master the big jumps!**

NATHAN: AN AMAZING LITTLE BOY

Nathan Oommen
Grade 1
Elizabeth Raju

Hi! My name is **Nathan**.

I am a Hoosier because I was born in Indiana.

My parents are immigrants from India.

My mom is a baker.

I am going to be seven on November 27th.

I love to eat healthy and exercise.

I am learning karate, and I love to sing and dance.

I also love to play around with my brother.

I love to spend time outside in nature.

My favorite restaurant is The Olive Garden.

Always active, smiling, and kind to all.

I AM CALEB FRYXELL

I am **Caleb**. I like chickens because they are fluffy and cute. I also like penguins, cats, dogs, and walruses. I like Kit-Kat candy bars because they are chocolatey and crunchy. I like to build fires and hatchets. I have a fort in the back yard. It is big. My favorite food is carbonara. I love my family. I love my mom because she lies in bed with me and reads my books. I love my dad because I get to watch YouTube in his bed. I have two brothers. I love them because I get to play soccer with them. I also love my Nana and Papa because I just do. **My heart makes me special. My heart makes me feel happy.**

This is a picture of my world.

ABOUT MY LIFE

Peyton Binns
Grade 1
Christal Binns

My name is **Haley Peyton Binns**, but I go by my middle name, Peyton. I guess that's a little different but it just shows I'm unique and pretty cool. I'm a first-grader at Oliver Ellsworth Elementary School in Windsor, Connecticut. I live with my mom, and my brother who sports a pretty cool mohawk and loves gaming as much as I do! Some people say girls shouldn't be gamers, but I don't think that's true. I think you can be whatever you put your mind to. If you believe it, you can achieve it!

I love hanging out with my family in my free time. We have weekly game nights where we try different board games. My favorite game is Monopoly. When I win, I get so excited I do a victory dance. It's fun being silly with my family. My mom is a nursing home administrator and loves working with her patients every day. She says it makes her happy to make a difference in the lives of others no matter how small. On some weekends we visit my Mema who is so much fun. She takes us out to lunch at my favorite restaurant, Chili's, and watches movies with us. My Mema is a nursing assistant and loves helping people, too! When I grow up, I want to help people and make a difference just like my mom and my Mema. **I will become a doctor and save lives. Dr. Binns! That sounds really cool!**

It's because we are different that each of us is special!

Eleanora Finkenstein
Grade 1
Zach Finkenstein

ME AND WHO I AM

This is my papa and my baby cousin.

My great-grandfather on my mother's side was the mayor of Windsor.

My papa (my dad's dad) makes carousels.

I love all animals. I want to work in animal rescue.

I want to be a ninja.

I want to be a geologist.

I want to be an artist.

SHE'S GOT THIS!

This is a picture of my little brother and me.

My name is **Mckenzie**. I am four years old.

I love my brother, Camden, and my mommy and my daddy. I am smart and strong. I like to read books. My favorite book is called *She's Got This!* My daddy reads it to me every night.

I love gymnastics! I like to go to school with my mommy. We're best girls!

My family likes to play outside, have bonfires, and snuggle in the mornings. I am proud!

COLTON, THE HAPPIEST BOY IN ALL THE LAND

Colton: The happiest boy in all the land, our biggest helper, our incredibly polite three-year-old with the most loving soul, our charmer yet wild child at heart.

In the mornings, Colton wakes up full of energy, jumps out of bed, and runs down the hall, busting our bedroom door open with a giant smile on his face like every day is "Trollstice." He must think, "Today is going to be the best day ever!"

Colton is the biggest helper, with no task too large to handle. You need the front door opened? He's got it. You need to take a sip of your water? Just sit back, and he will bring the glass of water to your mouth. To top it off, he then thanks you for letting him help. Can you imagine? A helper with amazing manners? That's Colton! He has the best manners, constantly repeating, "Thank you, Mommy. Thank you, Daddy."

Colton has the most loving soul and gives the best hugs, kisses, and snuggles, especially if mom or dad get hurt, or if his best friend, his sister, gets upset. He's right there with kisses to make everything better. As you can probably guess, he turns into quite the charmer when he wants something. Colton will walk up to us with the most devilish, adorable smile, clearly indicating he wants something he should not have. Yet how can we say no to those warm brown eyes looking up at us? Mom and dad are surely in trouble as he gets older.

This little man loves trains, cars, airplanes and all things sports. He's a climber and attempts to defy gravity while giving his mom a heart attack in the process. He is our Mr. Independent, our wild child. **When Colton grows up, he will be a force to be reckoned with.**

Colton: Mr Independent, wild child, a force to be reckoned with.

CREATIVITY

I like da song

Happier, making

Minecraft builds.

I'm always a fan

of *Minecraft*

videos, waiting for

another creative

challenge even if

it's hard. I like to

face stuff, like

making cool

builds in

Minecraft,

drawing awesome

places.

Edward Goins
Grade 1
Lucy Goins

I'm more special than a unicorn. In fact, I'm pretty much just a powerful ball of energy. I'm obsessed with the series called Dragonborn.

JUSTICE'S FAMILY

I am **Justice**.

We go to the zoo.

We like koalas. Sometimes we see them do flips.

We love lions. Everyone else gets scared, but I don't.

I love my family because they always care about anyone who gets hurt, and they never give up on anything, and **they always encourage me to do what I really want to do.**

I AM JACKSON

Hi! My name is **Jackson**, but my parents call me **Action Jackson** or **Jackie.** I am eight years old. I have three siblings—Abbie, Charley and Cole. I have a dog named Finley. My mom and dad surprised us with him last summer during quarantine. He is a Black Lab/German Shepherd mix. He is a smart dog and knows plenty of tricks. He's so smart he learned to sit and give a paw in one day! He loves to play ball and chase us around our back yard. My favorite thing to do is take walks with Finley and my family. We love taking him to Northwest Park and letting him play in the dog park. When he gets tired of playing, we take him on a trail. On the trail I love looking for salamanders and exploring the woods. Before leaving we visit all the animals and stop by the pond to watch the fish and catch tadpoles.

At home, I love to build forts with my siblings and work out with my mom. I like playing in my treehouse and going on the slide and swings. I love singing and dancing. It's especially fun when we have family dance parties. Last summer, Charley, Cole, and I put on a concert for our parents. It was so awesome! We had a concession stand, seating, and a stage that I built myself. I was the lead singer, Charley was the backup singer, and Cole was the guitarist. My parents loved it! My mom loved it so much she cried!

My favorite sports are basketball and baseball. I play baseball for Windsor Little League. Levi, my best friend from Pre-K, is on my team, so I'm so excited! I love pitching, and when my dad and I practice he tells me I "have quite the arm."

Jackson Moore
Grade 2
Katie Moore

Taking a walk with my siblings on a Saturday afternoon. It was so much fun!

On the weekends, I sometimes go to my Nema's house, a.k.a. my grandma's. I'm her first grandchild. When I was little, I couldn't say Grandma, so that's how she got the name Nema. I have so much fun at her house, and it's even more fun when my cousins are there.

I love learning, exploring, and telling facts. I especially love learning about reptiles, insects, animals, and the ocean. Did you know that albino animals have poor eyesight? Or that tarantulas use their hair as a weapon? They rub their hair on their prey and it feels like tiny daggers. Those are just a few of many fun facts that I can share with you. **And that's all about me! I hope you enjoyed my story!**

Keith Robinson Jr.
Grade 1
Tiwanna Robinson

RJ, MANY COLORS, MANY LAYERS

They call me **RJ.** RJ is for Robinson Jr., since I am named after my daddy. His name is Keith Robinson. I could have been called Junior, but my uncle is called that. I could have been called JR, or even KJ—my friend and another boy at my church have those names. My mom liked RJ, so RJ it was. That's what I've been called since I was born, but some people at my school call me Keith.

Like my name, I am different in so many ways. I like to run really fast like the Flash. I love to dance, sing my favorite songs, and play basketball, guitar, and the piano. I'm a *Pokémon* master, even though I am not ten yet! Some days, I'm the best martial artist: ninja, karate, you name it. My mom said she will teach me taekwondo. She's a third-degree Black Belt, but I think I can beat her. When I was one or two years old, she saw me kicking. She said that she noticed something special. So, she started teaching me how to kick, according to her, "the right way." But that didn't last long because I started kicking her all the time! I got a punching bag, and I just like sparring with her.

Now that I'm six, she said that she will teach me more. Who knows? I might grow up to be both a ninja and a *Pokémon* master!

Even though I like and do many things and people call me by different names, I am simply RJ.

Here I am doing a tae-kwon-do turning kick, striking my punching bag. Mom gave me a thumbs-up!

ALL ABOUT BROOKE

Brooke Petteway
Grade 1
Aisha S. Petteway

I am **Brooke**! I am often called Brooke Lynn or Brookie. In my story you are going to learn *a lot* about me and my family. First, let's start with me! It all began on a family trip to beautiful Puerto Rico. My mother came home with me in her tummy, is the story I am told. Anyway, now I am seven! I am energetic and compassionate, just like my mother. My favorite thing to do is play basketball, just like my father and my brothers. My favorite food is eggs, and I love sports. I just started playing baseball, like my brothers (dad never played). Well, I signed up for softball, but not enough girls signed up, probably because of the pandemic, but I don't mind playing baseball with the boys.

Guess what! This girl can dance, too. From ballet and jazz to hip-hop, I am what they call "the life of the party." Go Brooke Lynn, go Brooke Lynn!

On to my family. Fasten your seatbelt, because my family is *family*. I am the youngest of four. My brothers are Aaron (23) and Jarrell (17), and my sister is Chelsey (16). They are my everything! I watch everything they do and try to do it. I have a lot of cousins. I see my cousins every Christmas Eve at Grandma and Poppas; that's where the most fun happens. The coolest thing is one of my Poppas (Gil) lives in the same house as me. He is my father's father, and we love gardening together.

The best thing about my family is *all* my grandparents live near me, and I even have two great-grandmothers. My grandmas are my best friends. They love to dress me up and take me to church. The person I am most like is my dad. We are competitive. That's where my love for sports comes from. My dad played basketball in high school and college. I will do it, too.

The person I admire the most is my big sister, Chelsey. She is very pretty, smart, generous, and a fabulous dancer. Not to mention, she named me. She makes me be responsible, even when I am getting on her nerves. I tell her that's my job. My siblings and I love when our father laughs. It is pretty funny! We also love TACOOOOOO TUUUUEEEESDAY! Mom makes the best tacos (people say that's not really cooking, but we don't care).

I hope you enjoyed learning about me and my family. You should love us as much as I do by reading this story. I know it was a lot, and I believe there are more amazing stories to come.

Brookie Out!

This is a picture of my wonderful family at an awards ceremony. My father received the 100 Men of Color Award. He is awesome!

Gwendolyn Mitchell
Grade 1
Heather Mitchell

TO THE BEACH

The Mitchell mermaid family.

"Let's go to the beach," said Mom.

"OK," said Gwen.

"Get your things, Hayden. Get out here, Claire. Get off the iPad, Xbox, and TV. Get your bathing suits on if you want to go swimming!" said Mom. "Don't forget your swimmy, Hayden."

"Before we go swimming, I want to build a sandcastle with sand molds, sticks, seashells, and paper," said Gwen.

"I'll help," said Hayden.

"I want to go swimming really far out because it is shallow a lot of the time. I'll be swimming while you build your sandcastles," said Claire.

"Once we add the final details of a flag and then windows using a stick, Hayden and I will come swimming with you," said Gwen.

"And, when you're done, **I'll make all of you a mermaid tail out of sand.** It will be a lot of fun!" said Mom.

NATURALLY NOAH

Noah Lucey
Kindergarten
Evita Lucey

Hi, I'm Noah.

I'm six years old.

I'm in kindergarten.

I'll share some things, and I hope to make a connection with you.

I like to play with trains.

I like the color black.

I like to play with blocks to make a stack.

I like to run, run all around.

I like to play with my little sister and brother at the parks in our town.

I like to eat cookies, cake, and sometimes pie, but there's nothing I like more than my mommy's rice.

I am Noah.

This is me.

I am Noah, naturally.

This is me! Running all around on Easter.

WHO IS THIS GUY?

This is me at my sixth birthday party with my best friends and cousins Logan and Julia. Our family calls us "panos," which is their way of saying Primos, which is "cousins" in Portuguese.

I am **Sebastiao Bernardino**, but friends and family call me Sebby. I am one of three. You ask, "What does that mean?" Well, it means I am a triplet! I have two other brothers named Armando and Mateus. We were all born on the same day. I have a huge family. My family has many sets of twins, but we are the only triplets. My family ethnicity is Portuguese and Peruvian, which makes me trilingual. I speak English, Portuguese, and Spanish. My family is very united, and we often have celebrations so I see everyone all the time, especially in the summer. My cousin, Logan, has a pool so we see him all summer long, which makes me a very good swimmer.

I have many interests. I like to play and watch soccer, and my favorite soccer player is Cristiano Ronaldo. I play soccer at Windsor Rec and I play with my brothers. I like to watch motoGP with my father, and my favorite motorcycle rider is Marc Marquez. I hope one day to see a motoGP race in Austin, Texas.

When I play with my brothers I often pretend I am riding my bike like Marc Marquez and pass my brothers racing around the cul-de-sac. I love to win. That is why my favorite color is gold. When I grow up, I want to be a motorcycle rider just like Marc Marquez. Until then, I love going to school. My favorite subject is math, but I like to work on my reading in *Lexia*. I have been going to Oliver Ellsworth since Pre-K-3. OE is like a second home. It's such a good place to learn and get smart. **Thank you for reading about me.**

ME AND MY FAMILY

Madeline Leyden
Grade 2
Elizabeth Leyden

Hi! My name is **Maddie**. I was born on September 23, 2013. I am seven years old. I have a younger brother and sister; their names are Ben and Ellie. I have a mom, a dad, four grandparents, three great-grandparents, six aunts and uncles, four cousins, and one on the way in May! My family is part Irish. I love my family because they are so nice! My family always watches a movie and has pizza on Friday nights. It's the best night of the week!

I love to play outside with my siblings and friends. I live in a neighborhood with kids about my age. We all love to play together. This summer, my family is going on a road trip! Most summers we go to Maine, and we also go to visit my grandparents. When I grow up, I want to be a mom, a vet, and a teacher.

I love little kids and animals.

This is my family at Taughannock Falls in Ithaca, NY. We go here every summer.

Rosemary Stanton
Grade 2
Heather Stanton

A LITTLE ABOUT ME!

Hi, I'm **Rosemary**! My friends and family call me Rosey. I was born on July 29, 2013. I am half Scottish and a lot Irish! My parents are divorced. I live with my mom, brother, and dog, Pony Boy Curtis. I sleep at my dad's every Saturday night. On Friday nights we have movie night with my mom, brother, and of course Pony Boy.

A picture of me in one of my favorite places, the woods.

On Wednesdays, my brother and I go to my Nana's house for distance learning. I like school, but I hate waking up for it! I look forward to summer when we go on our yearly trip to Cape Cod.

My family has strong beliefs that *everyone* should be treated equally. We love people and helping people. My family tells me I can be anything I want to be when I grow up. **I want to be a singer.**

Maliyah Malcolm
Kindergarten
Debra Malcolm

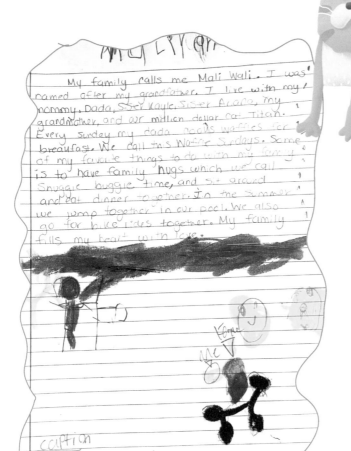

My family calls me Mali Wali. I was named after my grandfather. I live with my mommy, Dada, Sister Kayle, Sister Ariana, my grandmother, and our million dollar cat Titan. Every sunday my dada cooks waffles for breakfast. We call this Waffle Sundays. Some of my favorite things to do with my family is to have family hugs which we call Snuggie buggie time, and sit around and eat dinner together. In the summer, we jump together in our pool. We also go for bike rides together. My family fills my heart with love.

caption

Me and my sister riding bikes!

Me and my sister riding bikes.

HEART FULL OF LOVE

My family calls me **Mali Wali**. I was named after my grandfather. I live with my mommy, my dada, my sisters Kayle and Ariana, my grandma, and our million-dollar cat Titan.

Every Sunday my dad cooks waffles for breakfast. We call this Waffle Sundays. One of my favorite things to do with my family is to have family hugs which we call "snuggle buggie" time. We also sit and eat dinner together. In the summers, we jump in our pool together. We all go for bike rides together.

My family fills my heart with love.

Nick Carabai
Grade 1
Colleen

FUNNY BIG BROTHER

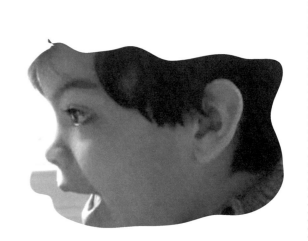

I am Nick Carabai, joke teller. I am seven years old and in first grade.

I am **Nick**! I am kind, creative and funny!

I love animals and want to become a zookeeper. Playing with my cousins is lots of fun! I love to make my family laugh. I put on shows for my family. I can make Gigi laugh by making funny faces. I love to read funny books! My mom and Nolan and I read the *Weird School* books. I tell jokes to Uncle Danny on FaceTime!

Mommy movie night is my favorite tradition!

I really, really want to get a dog!

Isaiah Louw
Kindergarten
Kaila Louw

The Buggy Book

The book that my son and I wrote its about bugs and animals becoming friends. Our book has illustrations of caterpillar's, bugs and different animals, that are all busy doing their work out in nature. While they are working, each one its trying to socialized and make friends. This book its to teach students of social skills, and difference's.

Author
Isaiah Louw
illustrated by: Mama

THE BUGGY BOOK

The book that my son and I wrote is about bugs and animals becoming friends.
Our book has illustrations of caterpillars, bugs, and different animals that are all busy doing their work out in nature. While they are working, each one is trying to socialize and make friends. This book is to teach students social skills and tolerance. While the bugs and animals are doing their work out in nature, they are also learning a lot about each other. **While they are in their own space and thinking of different things, deep inside they want to meet, play, and become friends.**

Wynter Golinski
Kindergarten
Juline Golinski

WYNTER: OUR SOUR PATCH KID

Wynter: Our sour patch kid, our sassy daughter whose personality is larger than life, our confident and ever-stylish fashionista, our drama princess and personal performer, and also our sweet child with such a gentle soul, especially when it comes to her brother.

Wynter loves people. Not just family. Not just close friends. She loves *everybody* and must tell them about her latest accomplishments or exciting gift she got for her birthday. Nothing is too small or out of the question to share. She is so full of love and affection, giving hugs to her family, friends and even her neighbors. Her greatest love is clearly her brother, though. She is always there for him with her most important task of giving kisses to take away any pain when he gets hurt. Even when they fight and her dad teasingly asks if we need to get rid of

her brother, she quickly jumps in with a powerful "NO!" showcasing just how much she loves him. They are truly the best of friends.

Wynter is our very own personal performer. She absolutely loves to dance and sing while dressing up as if every day is a dance recital or prom. We are so lucky that any money we spend on Halloween costumes will never go to waste! Most children wear a costume once, but Wynter will wear it until it comes apart at the seams. We knew we were in "trouble" when we saw her dance moves at the age of two while listening to her favorite artist, Lady Gaga.

It has been clear to us for the longest time that Wynter has a unique gift. She adores expressing herself through dance, costumes, and emotion. **We know she is bound to earn an Oscar in the future based on her dramatic performances in day-to-day life.**

Wynter Golinski, whose personality is larger than life.

I AM MARYA

I go outside a lot and play so much! I play with my siblings. My favorite food is noodles. They are so curly, like curly hair. My favorite color is light pink because it is so pale, and it is a beautiful color.

My favorite place is Six Flags because you can eat and go on fast rides! Some are slow, some are fast, but I love the fast ones. My favorite animal is a cat, and they are so soft to hold.

My favorite toy is Barbie because they are pretty and so fun to play with!

I love going outside because I love to play with my siblings. I'm going to get a trampoline. It's going to be fun!

I AM LEAH

My name is **Leah**. I like pasta. I also like sweaters. My brother, Dominic, likes bananas. He is two years old. We celebrated his birthday by having a party and making cupcakes. I like seeing my cousins. I love them. **I also have a new cousin.**

This is me, Leah!

I AM COLTON!

Colton Sperry
Pre-K
Kathleen Hudson

I am **Colton Frederick James Sperry**. I am named after my grandfather and my great-grandfather, and I think that's cool. I wish I got to meet my great-grandfather, though. I am the big brother to Lilyann and Ryder, and I love them very much. Even when Lilyann takes my stuff!

My family says that I am kind and sensitive. I just try to be nice to everyone. I like dinosaurs and Godzilla and King Kong. A lot! I am interested in all kinds of animals.

I have a lot of pets: a dog named Randy, my cat Boo-Boo, a turtle named Beans, and three Salamanders named Curly, Larry, and Moe.

That's who I am!

Quiet time.

THE ADDIE FIVE

We are the **Addie Five**. We work hard, play hard, and love hard. Our story began in college, and throughout several years and thousands of miles, we established new roots and were blessed with the three greatest gifts that life has to offer.

My daughters have eclectic personalities, but they have each other's backs and wear their hearts on their sleeves. Reese is our gymnast—fierce, determined and full of grace. Elena is our emotional songbird; she sings her way through her days, trying to add rhythm to her melodies and always telling us how much she loves everyone. Avery is our runner/fashionista; she only knows one speed when moving and that's *fast*! When she's not running, she wears any dress she can find and accessorizes to the best of her young ability.

My girls are tree-climbers, dirt-lovers and fancy outfit-wearing little ladies. Separately, we are all unique, but together, we are a cohesive unit. **Love binds us and always has since the beginning.**

Our "five" during the pandemic summer in one of our favorite outdoor spots.

GROWING UP ITALIAN

Miss Alexa D'Errico
First Grade Teacher

La cucina piccola fal la casa grande. A small kitchen makes the house big! Throughout most of my life, Sunday dinners were a time when everyone gathered at my grandmother's house for lots of food, laughter, and love. It was a place where we could just *be*.

The pasta with sauce and meatballs is more than just the food on our plate. Our meals represent love, empathy, hard work, and faith. Growing up Italian instilled the values of love, respect, and the importance of family. My grandparents had a revolving door, with so many family and friends coming in to enjoy a meal together. They showed their appreciation for others by cooking a warm meal for them.

Now, twenty years later, I strive to create a classroom community similar to my grandmother's dinner table. It's a place where all students feel loved and respected and have the opportunity to just *be*. Growing up Italian not only taught me how to cook a delicious meal for others, but to **make those around me feel loved by creating a recipe for shared success.**

Grandma Lorraine D'Errico with her pride and joy, her grandchildren. Alexa with her fiancé David (left), and Joe with his girlfriend Nicole (right). Grandma was so excited to feed two more grandchildren when Alexa and Joe brought David and Nicole to Sunday dinner.

Tressa Tedeschi
Kindergarten Teacher

Nonna making fresh homemade pasta. This was Nonna at her happiest!

NONNA-BUON APPETIT!

They say that food is what brings the family together. *Mangia, Mangia!* Eat, Eat! Those words echoed throughout my childhood while growing up in an Italian family. You never wanted to eat too fast because when your plate is empty, more food would be added to it. Sunday dinners were a staple at Nonna's house. All the cousins and families would make time to celebrate Nonna's cooking and the family being together.

Nonna would spend her days cooking, from morning to night. She had two refrigerators and two freezers one set of them in the upstairs kitchen and one in the garage kitchen. They had plenty of room to store all of our favorite foods. Those foods were like memories and good times. Each bite brought you back to a Sunday dinner when you spent time playing outside with your cousins or a time when the whole family was laughing together at the table during ravioli or meatball eating contests.

Thinking back to those Sunday dinners, the cousins never realized how much work and love was put into the food that was created. Our jobs were to play and sneak off into the freezers and steal frozen pasta. Our realization began to occur when we became adults. Spending time replicating Nonna's delicious ravioli or gnocchi has made us all see how much love she put into that food. **The food will never be the same as Nonnas, but I am so thankful for the memories she created for us,** and I hope one day my family and I can create those beautiful memories for my daughter.

Dawn Slaughter
Paraprofessional

FAMILY IS AN AMAZING THING

After a long day, it's nice to relax with my furry friends. (Dawn and Max, Sport and Coco)

Family is an amazing thing. My parents were loving and supportive, hardworking, and excellent role models. Their words were the law in our household. My brothers were the protectors. They tried their best to make sure their siblings were safe. They also encouraged us to be adventurous and not to shy away because of fear. My sisters worked hard to keep the house running smoothly when my parents were working. I can't forget our four-legged friends. My household was never without a dog. **There was a time when I had a dog and a pet squirrel!**

THE BARTHOLOMEW FAMILY

Anne Bartholomew
Kindergarten Teacher

Elliot, Greg, Courtney, Caster, and Paige

A long time ago, in a state far, far away (Pennsylvania), there lived a girl (Anne Bartholomew) who loved reading science fiction books and watching science fiction movies. She continued her love of this genre when she went to college. There, she met her future husband (Greg), also a science fiction fan.

Shortly after college graduation, Greg and I got married and joined the Peace Corps. We were assigned to the Philippines, where we lived for two years on the island of Bohol and learned the local language of Cebuano. It was a very exciting time in our lives, to learn a new language and culture. We joined the Peace Corps thinking we would help others. We soon learned that the Filipinos helped us more that we could ever help them. We are grateful to them.

Upon returning home, we started our own family. Courtney and Paige are our two daughters, and I am happy to say that they both enjoy science fiction. Over the years, our family has developed many traditions. One of our favorite traditions is to set up a regulation-sized badminton court in our back yard. We love playing. Our competition can get quite heated at times, but it is all in fun. Neighbors often join us, and this makes the competition more exciting.

Several years ago, Paige got married, and we are so lucky to have Elliot in our family. It is genuinely nice to finally have a son!

Our family has grown and changed over the years, but we remain close and enjoy being together.

My musical grandma, mom, dad, sister, brothers, husbands, wives, nieces, nephews, sons, daughters, and their spouses. I love you all!

Laurie Miller
First Grade Teacher

FAMILY LOVE SONG

Michelle Obama once said, "Music helps us share ourselves, our dignity and sorrows, our hopes and joys." My family was and is all about the music. Show tunes at my grandparent's house. My Dad playing classical piano and rock n' roll guitar. Folk group at church. Husband singing and playing everything from the blues and Hendrix to James Brown and the Beatles in local bands. Kicking back at summer "Concerts on the Windsor Green" with family, friends and neighbors. Outdoor Hartford Symphony concerts and Stevesong concerts at Roger Wolcott School. My daughter Carly loving Britney and the boy bands. Proudly attending my son Joe's college solo performances at the Hartt school. My students learning to sing "What a Wonderful World" and "Lift Ev'ry Voice and Sing" for class performances.

Like Michelle said, "Music allows us to hear one another, to invite each other in." It sure does!

Ben Eskenazi
Gym Teacher

Me with Laura, Layla, and Lena.

I AM ME BECAUSE OF THEM

My ancestors are from Poland, Greece, Turkey, and other Eastern European countries. I am the second son of Margaret and Steve, the older brother of Drew, and the little brother of Steve. I am me because of them.

My wife, Laura, is mostly Italian, but like me she also has ancestors from several countries. The only daughter of Carl and Estelle, she grew up with seven brothers and became the teacher she'd always dreamed of becoming. She is hardworking, caring, and the best wife and mother I could ever ask for. I am me because of Laura.

In April of 2018, we welcomed my daughter, Layla Mae, into the world. Smart, active and dramatic, she insists that I play with her all day long and then sing her songs at night before she goes to sleep. She will always be the little girl that made me a daddy. I am me because of Layla.

As if I wasn't already lucky enough, our second daughter, Lena Renee, was born in January of 2021. She sleeps straight through the night and when awake she is happy, attentive, and calm. She is obsessed with her momma and wants to watch her big sister's every move. I am me because of Lena.

I am so lucky and grateful for every one of these people for making me who I am. I am me because of them!

Many pictures of the members of my blended family!

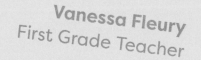

Vanessa Fleury
First Grade Teacher

BLENDED

Fleury, Miles, Shippa, Nason. These are the many family names that I carry. This is who I am. My family is what makes me whole. As a child, I grew up in two different households—my dad in one, my mom in the other. I thought it was pretty cool, especially because it meant that my brother and I would have two holiday celebrations! As I grew older, I watched my Mom and Dad fall in love with my bonus parents, also known as my step-parents. Now, I had even more family! I went from having one brother, who is my best friend, to having three brothers and three sisters. This made holidays and gatherings so much fun.

My family does a lot together. My grandparents always host a Sunday dinner at their house and cook delicious food for all of us to eat. In the summertime, we go camping together and have s'mores! My Papa takes us out on the river on his boat. We go tubing, fishing, and swimming. My Mimi and Papa are always looking for fun things to do with my cousins and me. My Papa taught me how to play basketball. He used to take me to the school he coached at and let me practice with his team. My Mimi and I both love the beach. We even have small beach-themed tattoos! My mom is the most caring, thoughtful, wise woman I know. She always made sure that my brother and I were taken care of, even when she was having a bad day. She is my hero. I am who I am today because of her.

My family is my rock. They are kind, funny, caring, honest, and unique. **A blended family is a happy family.**

Taran Gruber
Principal

URBAN COMMUNE

The Gruber family is about community, as a family unit and beyond. Growing up in an urban commune was, for me and my sister, the foundation on which everything was built and then passed on to our own children. Every day, fifteen to thirty people were served dinner, with all contributing to the cooking, shopping, or cleaning up. Occasional and some regular guests were always welcomed—and put to work. Dinner discussion was filled with vibrant language and dissension while enjoying a traditional meal we called Gruber A La Spam (sauteed Spam with LeSeur peas and red cabbage, plus a dash of secret seasoning). There was always music during dinnertime: rock, folk, pop, classical, an eclectic mix. Children and adults alike were heard and respected on topics ranging from politics, education, and justice to just how to handle the daily issues of life. We also pondered how our German heritage impacted our desire to work with our hands (gardening and woodwork) and our longing for traditions.

To this day, small talk is something we awkwardly try to participate in but never do well. We attended Hartford public schools, never considering private schools or moving as many of our white neighbors did. Diversity was the point. Although I now live outside of Hartford, it was crucial in my heart and mind to send our twins, Kendra and Cameron, to a school in Hartford. My soul warms, and I feel at peace, when I attend functions at Batchelder Montessori in Hartford with my twins. Its being a Montessori-modeled school was of little importance to me. I knew, from firsthand experience, the enormous importance of learning and growing with people who did not look like me, did not worship like me, did not dance like me—but **did love just like me.**

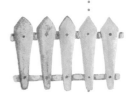

Our commune began in Rockville with members moving from NYC, Boston, and D.C. We stayed at this house for a few years before finding our permanent location in Hartford, Connecticut.

GREEK EASTER

Stacy Marcella
Kindergarten Teacher

My family would celebrate Greek Easter when I was growing up. At the dinner table, each family member would have a red hard-boiled egg. The youngest would tap an end of their egg against the oldest family member's egg. The game would continue until the person with the last surviving, uncracked egg was deemed the winner for that year. We would say this person would be lucky all year long. **After sharing this story, I learned that other cultures have a similar tradition.**

Greek Easter egg tapping game.

Christina Chapple
Kindergarten Teacher

ME IS WE

My ginormous, energetic, passionate, fun-loving family. from Philly to Jersey to florida to Nigeria, and back again.

I am Me, but Me is WE.

We are a ginormous, energetic, passionate, fun-loving family. We are multicultural. We are multilingual. We are intelligence, wit, bravery, and excellence personified. We are generations of strength, perseverance, ingenuity, and kind-heartedness.

We are backyard barbeques, snacking on the culinary delights of our matriarch. The whole neighborhood calls her Granny. We are epic Nigerian feasts, prepared with love, spice, and culture. There is no jollof rice and puff-puff quite like ours!

We are family game nights, from "inventing" new scrabble words to exchanging "the eye" during a game of spades. We are raw comedy, from laughing until we cry, to movie quotes and family catchphrases. We are eloquent, intense conversations, from defending our football teams to conversing about any topic under the sun. Some call us fast-talking, but we call it "that east coast twang."

We are tenacious; our connection, love, and persistence to be our best selves is unshakeable. We are positivity and optimism; we gather over meals, holding hands because in the presence of good food and family, there's no obstacle that we can't overcome. Just don't let Unc bless the food, or you'll be waiting quite a while before you eat. We are every beautiful thing and without WE, there is simply no Me.

So you see, Me is WE. My family, WE, are our ancestors' wildest dreams come true!

THIS IS WHAT SUCCESS LOOKS LIKE!

Lorretta Satchell
Paraprofessional

I am now the woman that the public school said I could not be. I was told that I should consider a trade because I was not college material. Colleage was my dream! Today I am a college graduate. I am a proud daughter, wife, mother, sister, aunt, and friend. In addition, I am a great employee and a business owner.

The most important things to me are my relationship with God, my family, and my commitment to being the best!

My family is extraordinary. My husband, my children, and my work are my reasons why—why I love, why I live, why I strive to want more and to be the best!

My story simply says never give up on your dreams, because dreams really do come true.

Dreams really do come true.

ON THE MOVE

Hello, everyone! My name is **Mr. Dowd**, and I am the P.E. teacher at Oliver Ellsworth. I absolutely love my job and all the kids I am lucky enough to teach every day. When I am not at school, I coach hockey and baseball at Windsor High School!

My family has always been super important to me. I grew up with my two parents, and I am the middle of three boys. Growing up in my house was so much fun. My brothers and I were *always* playing games in and outside our house. Sometimes we drove our parents crazy, but it was in good fun. Sometimes we would even make them play our games with us! I think my background of being outside so much and playing games and sports made me want to be a P.E. teacher!

I love to be active, and I can thank my brothers and parents for my love of physical activity!

Chris Williams
Behavior Technician

BEING BLACK

To be Black is to be on the defense all the time. Being Black means you probably didn't learn about your history and culture growing up. Being Black means you had to prove yourself whether at work, sport, or just having an intellectual conversation. Being Black is like running a never-ending marathon against racism. Being Black means pointing out injustices and lack of inclusion and then being told you're overreacting or, even worse, just imagining things. Being Black means that your hairstyle often did not fit the look of the company. Being black means "talking less Black," whatever that means.

Being Black means that a twelve-year-old boy playing with a toy gun in the park is a death sentence at the hands of the police within four seconds. Being Black means you are African, African American, Black American or simply Black with no nationality. Being Black means your ancestors were kidnapped and brought to a foreign land, enslaved, taught the ways of their oppressor, denied basic rights, and then looked at as lazy and unable to learn, and treated as a piece of property.

Being Black meant you couldn't sit at the lunch counter or drink from a particular water fountain and couldn't sit in the front of the bus. Being Black means we have to have the talk with our kids about how to conduct themselves when they are pulled over by the police. Being Black means living in a White America and still having to tell them my Black life matters.

My beautiful family.

MY AMAZING FAMILY

My name is **Lindsey Majors**, and I'm the youngest of three daughters. My mother and father are amazing human beings. They've taught me many valuable life lessons. Growing up, I always felt loved and understood by them. I always had someone cheering me on in everything I attempted to do. They encouraged me to follow my dreams, even when the world said no. When I wanted to be a scientist, my parents supported me. When I wanted to be a stunt double for movies, they supported me. No matter how big or small my dreams were, they made them feel important and reachable.

My biggest influence in my life has been my grandparents. They taught me the importance of love— love for myself, love for others, and love for creatures big and small. Except spiders. Never spiders.

My favorite memories are sailing across Block Island with Mimi, Pop, Mom, Dad, Emily, and Jennifer around me. We would always go to the sandbar and pick up the most beautiful shells. My other set of grandparents, Dodie and Grandpa, would invite us up to New Hampshire where we would drive around the mountains and find small shops to explore. Without all their guidance, I would not be the woman I am today. I am strong, adventurous, happy, and loving because of my family's influence. **I love them more than Baby Yoda—and that's saying a lot.**

COCO-CATASTROPHE

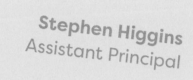
Stephen Higgins
Assistant Principal

The ideals of beauty in the American culture have not been able to amplify the construction of beauty that is called Coco-Catastrophe. My three daughters, Téa, Layla, and Nia represent the perfectly imperfect model of the many possibilities of a woman of color in America. The ingredients that make their Coco is unique to who they are, the things they like, and how they see their reflection in the world.

Téa's (11) Coco is made of one-half determination and one-half power. She walks with confidence and demands reasoning, understanding, and patience, even from her own dad. She is fiercely competitive and loves a great challenge. She is caring, and her heart is pure. She wants to become a professional athlete.

The second part of Coco-Catastrophe is Layla. She is three-fourths creativity and one-fourth emotion. She loves to be around people. Layla has the warmest smile, is a master jokester, and a natural leader. She has a strong sense of independence, loves to snowboard, and will become an actress one day.

Nia. Ohhhhhh, Nia. Nia is one-half determination, one-fourth compassion, and one-fourth unpredictable. She loves—I mean *loves*—animals. She has to do everything herself, and please, do not get in her way. I'm just saying, it could get dangerous. Unless you're an animal. Then you are OK.

Coco Catastrophe in full effect! This is Layla, Téa, and Nia, my beautiful three that bring me all the happiness in the world! Lucky dad.

Coco-Catastrophe is life! These three girls model some of the many possibilities of brown girls in the world. Their ingredients cannot be replicated, only appreciated. I'm looking for you to help me, to recognize their model of beauty for the greater cause: **Black and Brown Excellence and Beauty.**

We hope you have enjoyed reading this collection, and learning more about the incredible students and families of Oliver Ellsworth School.

If you are interested in having Publish Your Purpose Press produce a similar book project for you and your school district, please contact hello@publishyourpurposepress.com.

PUBLISH YOUR PURPOSE® PRESS

CPSIA information can be obtained
at www.ICGtesting.com
Printed in the USA
BVRC101151280821
615328BV00033B/46